Especially for

....

From

....

Date

....

Compiled by MariLee Parrish.

ISBN 978-1-60260-984-6

Published by Barbour Publishing, Inc., P.O. Box 719, Uhrichsville, Ohio 44683, www.barbourbooks.com

Our mission is to publish and distribute inspirational products offering exceptional value and biblical encouragement to the masses.

Member of the
Evangelical Christian
Publishers Association

Printed in China.

365

Decadent Dishes for

Chocolate

Lovers

BARBOUR
PUBLISHING

Day 1

Chocolate Eggnog
• • • • • • • • • • • • • • • •

1 egg
2 teaspoons chocolate syrup
2 teaspoons sugar
2 tablespoons crushed ice
1½ cups milk

Blend all ingredients together. Serve.

Day 2

Banana Bars
. . . .

¾ cup butter, softened
1 cup brown sugar
1 egg
3 ripe bananas
½ teaspoon cinnamon
½ teaspoon salt
4 cups quick oats
½ cup chocolate chips

*In large mixing bowl, cream together butter
and sugar. Add egg, bananas, cinnamon, and salt.
Mix well. Add remaining ingredients and mix.
Spread into greased 13x9-inch pan. Bake for 45 to 50
minutes or until a toothpick comes out clean.
Allow bars to cool before cutting into squares.*

Day 3

Basic Food Groups
. . . .

There are four basic food groups—
milk chocolate, dark chocolate, white
chocolate, and chocolate truffles.

UNKNOWN

Day 4

Chocolate Glaze
. . . .

Beat 1 cup powdered sugar, 1 tablespoon water,
1 ounce melted unsweetened chocolate (cool),
and 1 teaspoon vanilla until smooth.
Stir in water, 1 teaspoon at a time,
until frosting reaches desired consistency.
Use on cookies, cakes, and donuts.

Day 5

Chocolate Banana Smoothie
. . . .

1 cup crushed ice
2 large bananas
1½ cups milk
¼ cup vanilla yogurt
3 tablespoons chocolate
instant breakfast mix

Place the ice in the bottom of a blender.
Add remaining ingredients. Puree until smooth.
Serve immediately.

Day 6

Devil's Food Cake Cookies
. . . .

½ cup butter, softened
3 ounces cream cheese, softened
1 egg
1 (18 ounce) package devil's food cake mix
1½ cups semisweet chocolate chips, divided

*Beat together butter, cream cheese, and egg.
Add cake mix and mix well. Stir in 1 cup
chocolate chips. Roll dough into balls and
place on ungreased cookie sheet. Press down
on each ball with a glass to flatten. Bake at 375
degrees for 7 to 9 minutes. Cool for 2 minutes,
then remove from cookie sheet to cool
completely. Melt remaining chocolate chips
and drizzle over cooled cookies.*

Day 7

Black Forest Mocha
• • • • • • • • • • • • • •

⅔ cup hot brewed coffee
2 tablespoons chocolate syrup
2 tablespoons light cream
1 tablespoon maraschino cherry juice
Whipped topping

*In large mug, stir together coffee, syrup,
cream, and cherry juice. Garnish with
whipped topping. Serve immediately.*

Day 8

Easy Microwave Fudge
. . . .

2 cups semisweet chocolate chips
1 cup milk chocolate chips
1 (14 ounce) can sweetened condensed milk
1 teaspoon vanilla

*In large microwavable bowl, combine
chocolate chips and sweetened condensed milk.
Microwave on high for 2 minutes.
Add vanilla. Stir. Line 8x8 pan with
waxed paper and pour in fudge. Refrigerate.*

Day 9

Chocolate Ice-Cream Balls

· · · · · · · · · · · · · · · · · · · ·

3 cups chocolate ice cream
15 chocolate sandwich cookies, crushed
1½ cups semisweet chocolate chips
½ cup milk chocolate chips, melted

*Using ice-cream scoop, scoop ice-cream
mixture into six balls. Roll in crushed cookies.
Place on cookie sheet lined with waxed paper
and freeze for 2 hours or until firm.
Place frozen ice-cream balls on wire rack.
Spoon melted chocolate over each ball. Freeze
again until firm, at least 1 hour. Remove from
freezer 10 minutes before serving.*

Day 10

Oatmeal Kiss Freezer Cookies
· ·

1 cup butter, softened, no substitutions
1 cup powdered sugar
⅛ teaspoon salt
1 teaspoon vanilla
1¼ cups flour
1 cup quick oats
Chocolate Kiss candies

Cream together butter, sugar, salt, and vanilla.
Stir in flour and oats. Shape dough into
2 long rolls, each 1½ inches diameter.
Wrap in waxed paper. Chill for at least
2 hours or freeze for up to 3 months.

Day 11

Chocolate Dip
· · · · · · · · · · ·

2 cups cream cheese, softened
½ cup whipped topping
½ cup mini chocolate chips
½ teaspoon vanilla
¼ cup brown sugar
1 teaspoon cinnamon
Cinnamon for dusting
Graham crackers

In bowl, beat cream cheese and whipped topping until smooth. Add chocolate chips and vanilla; mix well. Blend in brown sugar and cinnamon. Garnish with light dusting of cinnamon. Serve with graham crackers at room temperature.

Day 12

Healthy Oatmeal Cookies

- - - - - - - - - - - - - - - - - - - -

2 cups brown sugar
3 cups wheat flour
2 teaspoons salt
2 teaspoons soda
1 teaspoon baking powder
6 cups rolled oats
2 cups applesauce
2 eggs
2 teaspoons vanilla

Mix dry ingredients. Add applesauce, eggs, and vanilla. Mix well. Drop by teaspoonfuls onto greased baking sheet. Bake at 350 degrees for about 10 to 12 minutes. Can add raisins or chocolate chips.

Day 13

Raspberry Truffle Latte
. . . .

6 ounces hot brewed coffee
2 tablespoons chocolate syrup
2 tablespoons raspberry syrup
½ cup (4 ounces) chocolate ice cream
Whipped topping
Grated chocolate
Fresh raspberries

*Mix coffee and flavored syrups in mug.
Spoon ice cream into coffee mixture. Add whipped
topping, grated chocolate, and fresh raspberries
as desired. Makes 1 mug.*

Day 14

White Cereal Mix
· · · · · · · · · · · · · · ·

1 (12 ounce) package semisweet
chocolate chips
½ cup butter
1 cup peanut butter
1 box corn cereal squares
2 cups powdered sugar

*Melt chocolate chips, butter, and peanut
butter together. Stir in cereal and coat well.
In large clean plastic bag, combine powdered
sugar and cereal. Tie bag closed and
shake to completely coat.*

Day 15

More Chocolate!
. . . .

A good chocolate drink could always use. . .more chocolate! Custom-make your own stirring spoons. Dip a plastic spoon into melted chocolate. Allow it to set slightly, resting on waxed paper, then fill the spoon bowl with more melted chocolate. When the chocolate is cooled and completely set, you can wrap the spoons in plastic wrap and share them with other chocolate lovers.

FROM *STIRRIN' UP CHOCOLATE & JOY*

Day 16

Cake Mix Cookies
. . . .
1 box chocolate cake mix
½ cup vegetable oil
2 eggs
1 cup white chocolate chips

Preheat oven to 350 degrees. Combine all ingredients in bowl and mix well with spoon. Drop by heaping tablespoons onto ungreased cookie sheet. Bake for 8 to 10 minutes. Do not overbake. Remove to wire rack to cool.

Day 17

Seven-Layer Bars
. . . .

½ cup butter or margarine
1 cup graham cracker crumbs
1 cup semisweet chocolate chips
1 cup butterscotch chips
1 cup chopped walnuts
1 cup shredded coconut
1 (14 ounce) can sweetened condensed milk

*Preheat oven to 350 degrees. In 9x13-inch
baking dish, cut butter and melt in oven. Remove
dish before butter turns brown. Sprinkle
graham cracker crumbs on top. Pat down.
Scatter chips, nuts, and coconut in layers on top.
Drizzle with condensed milk. Bake for
30 minutes or until light brown.*

Day 18

Brownie Bites
· · · · · · · · · · · ·

1 (15 ounce) package brownie mix
⅓ cup hot water
¼ cup applesauce
1 egg
48 mini peanut butter cups

*Preheat oven to 350 degrees. Combine
brownie mix, water, applesauce, and egg in bowl;
mix well. Fill paper-lined mini muffin cups about
half full. Press peanut butter cup into each cup.
Bake for 15 to 20 minutes. Remove from
muffin pans and place on wire rack to cool.*

Day 19

Peanut Butter Chocolate Chip Cake Mix Cookies
. . . .

2 eggs
⅓ cup water
¼ cup softened butter
1 cup peanut butter
1 package vanilla cake mix
1 (12 ounce) package chocolate chips

Preheat oven to 375 degrees. Beat eggs, water, butter, and peanut butter with electric beaters and half the cake mix until light and fluffy. Stir in remaining cake mix and chocolate chips. Drop by rounded teaspoonfuls on ungreased baking sheet. Bake 10 to 12 minutes.

Day 20

Kristy's Triple Chip Wonder Cookies
. . . .

1 box white cake mix
1 stick butter or margarine, melted
2 eggs
½ cup white chocolate chips
½ cup butterscotch chips
½ cup semisweet chocolate chips

*Mix cake mix with melted butter and eggs.
Stir in chips. Drop by spoonful onto ungreased
cookie sheet. Bake for 6½ minutes at
350 degrees. Oven times may vary
depending on your oven. Don't overcook;
the cookies will set up as they cool.*

Day 21

Caramel Chocolate Cappuccino
. . . .

1 cup hot water
¾ cup milk
2 tablespoons chocolate syrup
3 tablespoons caramel syrup
1 tablespoon instant coffee granules

*Place all ingredients in microwavable bowl
and microwave on high for 3 minutes or until hot.
Stir and pour into mugs. Serve immediately.*

Day 22

Snow Fudge
. . . .

2 cups sugar
1 cup evaporated milk
½ cup butter
1 cup white chocolate chips
½ cup flaked coconut
½ cup coarsely chopped pecans
1 teaspoon vanilla

*In heavy 3-quart saucepan, cook sugar,
evaporated milk, and butter over medium
heat to 238 degrees, stirring constantly.
Remove from heat. Allow mixture to stand
without stirring for 10 minutes. Add white
chocolate chips. Beat until melted. Quickly stir
in coconut, pecans, and vanilla. Pour into
buttered 8x8-inch pan. Cool. Cut into squares.*

Day 23

Chocolate Nut Chews
. . . .

1½ cups sugar
¼ cup cocoa
½ cup evaporated milk
⅓ cup butter
⅓ cup peanut butter
1 teaspoon vanilla
1½ cups quick oats
½ cup cashews

*In heavy 2-quart saucepan, mix sugar,
cocoa, evaporated milk, and butter. Stir over
medium heat until mixture boils. Boil and stir
for 2 minutes more. Remove from heat. Stir in
peanut butter until melted; add vanilla, oats,
and cashews. With 2 teaspoons, drop onto
waxed paper. Let stand until set.*

Day 24

Chocolate Walnut Puffs

1 cup semisweet chocolate chips
2 egg whites
Dash salt
½ cup sugar
½ teaspoon vanilla
½ teaspoon vinegar
¾ cups chopped peanuts

Preheat oven to 350 degrees. In double boiler, melt chocolate chips. In bowl, beat egg whites until foamy. Add salt. Gradually add sugar and beat until stiff peaks form. Add vanilla and vinegar. Fold in melted chocolate chips and peanuts. Drop by teaspoons onto greased cookie sheet. Bake for 10 to 12 minutes.

Day 25

Chocolate Bread
. . . .

2½ cups flour
1½ teaspoons baking soda
½ cup cocoa
1 cup sugar
1 egg, beaten
⅓ cup butter, melted
1¼ cups milk
¾ cup chopped walnuts

Preheat oven to 350 degrees. In large mixing bowl, sift together flour, baking soda, cocoa, and sugar. In smaller bowl, mix together egg, butter, and milk. Pour wet ingredients into dry ingredients; mix well. Fold in walnuts. Pour into greased 5x9-inch loaf pan. Bake for 1 hour.

Day 26

Easy Mini Cheesecakes

1 dozen vanilla wafers
2 (8 ounce) packages cream cheese
1 teaspoon vanilla
½ cup sugar
2 eggs
Chocolate syrup

Line muffin pan with 12 foil liners.
Place a vanilla wafer in each liner. In a mixing
bowl, combine cream cheese, vanilla, and sugar.
Beat well. Add eggs and beat until well blended.
Pour cream cheese mixture over wafers.
Fill each liner about ¾ full. Bake at 325 degrees
for 25 minutes. Garnish with chocolate syrup.

Day 27

Easy Chocolate Peanut Butter Pie

⅓ cup peanut butter
¾ cup powdered sugar
1 (9 inch) baked pie shell
½ cup chocolate chips
1 large box vanilla pudding,
prepared according to package directions
2 cups whipped topping

*In a small bowl use a pastry blender
to combine peanut butter and powdered sugar;
set aside. Line baked pie shell with ⅓ of peanut
butter mixture and chocolate chips. Make one
large box of vanilla pudding, and place on
top of peanut butter mixture. Cool. Top with
2 cups of whipped topping and sprinkle
remaining peanut butter mixture
over entire top of pie. Chill well.*

Day 28

White Chocolate
Raspberry Mocha

. . . .

1 cup milk
4 tablespoons white chocolate chips
1 cup of brewed espresso
1 teaspoon raspberry syrup
Whipped topping

Heat milk in a saucepan over low heat.
Stir in chocolate chips until melted.
Add coffee and syrup. Stir. Pour into
mugs and top with whipped topping.

Day 29

Stress Relief
· · · · · · · · · ·

When you find yourself feeling overly
stressed, curl up in your favorite chair
with a steaming mug of hot chocolate,
complete with loads of whipped topping,
and read through your favorite portion of
scripture. You'll be more joyful for it!

FROM *STIRRIN' UP CHOCOLATE & JOY*

Day 30

Brownie Pizza
. . . .

1 (15 ounce) package fudge brownie mix
½ cup peanut butter
½ cup mini chocolate chips
1 (6 ounce) package candy-coated
milk chocolate pieces

*Grease a 12-inch pizza pan. Prepare brownie
mix according to instructions and press onto the
pizza pan. Bake at 350 degrees for 15 minutes
or until done in center. Remove from the oven and
let sit 2 minutes. Drop peanut butter and mini
chips onto brownie and let sit for 30 seconds
or until peanut butter is melted and easily
spreadable. Spread over brownie
and top with candy pieces.*

Day 31

Puppy Chow
. . . .

1 cup chocolate chips
½ cup peanut butter
¼ cup butter
¼ teaspoon vanilla
9 cups toasted oat cereal
1½ cups powdered sugar

Combine chocolate chips, peanut butter, and butter in a bowl. Microwave on high 1 to 1½ minutes or until smooth, stirring after 1 minute. Stir in vanilla. In a large bowl, pour mixture over cereal, stirring until all pieces are evenly coated. Place cereal mixture and sugar in a large resealable plastic bag. Shake until all pieces are well coated. Spread on waxed paper to cool. Store in a resealable plastic bag.

Day 32

No-Bake Delights
. . . .

2 cups sugar
3 tablespoons unsweetened cocoa
½ cup margarine
½ cup milk
⅛ teaspoon salt
3 cups quick oats
½ cup peanut butter
1 teaspoon vanilla

*In heavy saucepan bring sugar, cocoa,
margarine, milk, and salt to a rapid boil
for 1 minute. Add quick oats, peanut butter,
and vanilla, and mix well. Working quickly,
drop by spoonful onto waxed paper and let cool.*

Day 33

Rich Parisian Chocolate
. . . .

1 cup whole milk
¾ cup heavy cream
¼ cup sugar
5 ounces semisweet chocolate, chopped
Whipped topping

*In saucepan over medium-high heat,
bring milk, cream, and sugar to a simmer
(heating just until bubbles appear around edges
of liquid). Remove from heat and add chocolate,
stirring until mixture is smooth. If necessary,
return pan to low heat while stirring with
a wooden spoon until chocolate is melted.
Serve in small mugs with whipped topping.*

Day 34

It's Good!
· · · · · · · · ·

Chocolate...
More chocolate...
A little more chocolate...
Life is good!

FROM STIRRIN' UP CHOCOLATE & JOY

Day 35

Chocolate-Drizzled Kettle Corn

· ·

Pop several bags of microwave
kettle corn and place in a large baking pan.
Take ½ cup chocolate chips and
microwave on high for 30 seconds.
Stir. Repeat until chips are melted.
Take a fork and dip into the chocolate.
Drizzle the chocolate over the kettle corn.

Day 36

Crunchy Chocolate Cookies

. . . .

1 cup chow mein noodles
2 cups mini marshmallows
2 cups oatmeal
1 (12 ounce) package chocolate chips
1 (12 ounce) package peanut butter chips

*Combine noodles, marshmallows, and oatmeal
in a large bowl. Stir. In a separate bowl,
microwave chips for 1 to 2 minutes or until
melted. Pour over noodle mixture and stir to coat.
Spoon clumps onto waxed paper and cool.*

Day 37

Chocolate Chip Pancakes
· · · · · · · · · · · · · · · · · · · ·

2 cups flour
¼ cup sugar
2 tablespoons baking powder
2 eggs
1½ cups milk
¼ cup vegetable oil
½ cup mini chocolate chips

In bowl, combine flour, sugar, and baking powder.
In separate bowl, combine eggs, milk, and oil;
add to dry ingredients and mix well.
Stir in chocolate chips. Pour batter by ¼ cupfuls
onto lightly greased hot griddle. Turn when
bubbles form on top. Cook until second side
is golden brown. Serve warm.

Day 38

Chocolate Hazelnut Coffee
. . . .

¾ cup hot water

¼ cup hot milk

2 teaspoons hazelnut-flavored
instant coffee granules

1 teaspoon cocoa

1 tablespoon dark brown sugar

1 tablespoon whipped topping

*Stir together all ingredients except
whipped topping. Pour into mugs. Top with
whipped topping and serve immediately.*

Day 39

Surprise Kisses
. . . .

1 cup butter, softened
½ cup granulated sugar
1½ teaspoons vanilla
1¾ cups flour
1 cup finely chopped pecans
1 (7 ounce) bag chocolate
Kiss candies, unwrapped
Powdered sugar

*Cream together butter, granulated sugar,
and vanilla. Blend in flour and chopped pecans.
Wrap one tablespoon of dough around each
chocolate candy Kiss. Bake at 350 degrees for
about 15 minutes, or until dough is set but not
browned. Roll each cookie in powdered sugar
while still warm. Makes 2 to 3 dozen cookies.*

Day 40

Chocolate Gravy and Biscuits
. . . .

½ cup milk
½ cup flour
½ cup sugar
1 tablespoon cocoa
1 teaspoon vanilla
¼ cup butter
1 tube refrigerated biscuits, baked

*Bring milk to a near boil in saucepan
and add flour, sugar, cocoa, and vanilla.
Stir constantly with whisk until thick. Then
add butter and whip to make gravy smooth
and creamy. Pour over warm biscuits.*

Day 41

Jeanne's Chocolate Chip Cookies
. . . .

½ cup butter
½ cup shortening
1 cup brown sugar
½ cup white sugar
1 teaspoon vanilla
1 teaspoon water

2 beaten eggs
3¼ cups flour
1 teaspoon baking soda
1 teaspoon salt
16 ounces chocolate
  chips

*Cream butter, shortening, sugars, vanilla,
and water until fluffy. Add eggs and mix well.
Stir in flour, soda, and salt until mixed well.
Add chocolate chips. Bake 10 to 12 minutes or
until edges are golden brown. Remove from
pan and cool completely. Makes about 4 dozen.*

Day 42

Chocolate Fruit Salad
. . . .

1 small box instant vanilla pudding mix
1 cup buttermilk
1 (8 ounce) can fruit cocktail, drained
1 (8 ounce) can crushed pineapple, drained
1 cup mini marshmallows
1 (8 ounce) container frozen
whipped topping, thawed
16 fudge-striped cookies, crushed

Combine pudding mix and buttermilk.
Add drained fruit cocktail and crushed pineapple.
Stir in marshmallows, whipped topping,
and crushed cookies. Chill.

Day 43

Walnut Balls
• • • • • • • • • • •

1 cup butter
⅓ cup brown sugar
1 teaspoon vanilla
2 cups flour
½ teaspoon salt

1½ cups finely chopped walnuts
Powdered sugar
½ cup chocolate chips

Preheat oven to 375 degrees. Cream butter, sugar, and vanilla until fluffy. Sift flour and salt together; add to creamed mixture. Mix well; stir in walnuts. Shape dough into walnut-sized balls. Bake on ungreased cookie sheet for 12 to 15 minutes. Remove from cookie sheet. When still warm but cool enough to handle, roll in powdered sugar. Melt chocolate chips and drizzle over walnut balls.

Day 44

White Chocolate Coffee
. . . .
3 ounces white chocolate, grated
2 cups whole milk
2 cups hot brewed coffee
Whipped topping (optional)

Place grated white chocolate and milk in microwavable bowl and heat for 2 minutes; stir until mixture is smooth and chocolate is melted completely. Stir in coffee. Serve in large mugs and garnish with whipped topping.

Day 45

Chocolate Delight Cake
. . . .

½ cup butter	1 teaspoon baking soda
½ cup sugar	¼ teaspoon cinnamon
2 eggs	¼ teaspoon salt
1¾ cups cake flour	1 cup milk
½ cup cocoa	1 teaspoon vanilla

Preheat oven to 350 degrees. Cream together butter and sugar until light and fluffy. Add eggs, beating after each addition. Sift together flour, cocoa powder, baking soda, cinnamon, and salt. Add half of flour mixture to egg mixture. Add milk and vanilla. Then stir in remaining flour mixture. Bake for 25 to 30 minutes in greased baking pan.

Day 46

A Sweet Aroma
. . . .

Chocolate and coffee go well together.
Create a welcoming atmosphere in your home
by placing an aromatic candle—vanilla is a
good choice—in a bowl or jar. Fill the space
around the candle with whole coffee beans up
to an inch from the top of the candle. Then
drink coffee and eat chocolate by candlelight.

FROM STIRRIN' UP CHOCOLATE & JOY

Day 47

Aunt Jo's Brownies
. . . .

2 eggs
1 cup granulated sugar
½ teaspoon salt
1 teaspoon vanilla
⅓ cup shortening, melted
2 ounces unsweetened
chocolate squares, melted
¾ cup flour
1 cup chopped walnuts

*Beat eggs lightly with spoon. Stir in sugar,
salt, and vanilla. Add shortening and chocolate.
Stir in flour and walnuts. Spread mixture
into greased 8-inch square pan. Bake at
325 degrees for about 30 minutes.*

Day 48

Éclair Cake
. . . .

1 box graham crackers
4 cups milk
2 small boxes instant vanilla pudding mix
1 (16 ounce) container frozen
whipped topping, thawed
1 (16 ounce) tub prepared chocolate frosting

*Line bottom of 9x13-inch baking pan with
graham crackers. In large bowl, combine milk and
pudding mix prepared according to directions on
box. Fold in whipped topping. Spread layer of
pudding mixture over graham crackers. Alternate
graham cracker and pudding layers to top of pan.
In microwave, cook tub of prepared frosting,
uncovered, for 1 minute on medium heat.
Pour over cake. Refrigerate for at least
12 hours before serving.*

Day 49

Chocolate Shortbread
· · · · · · · · · · · · · · · · · · · ·

1 cup butter, softened
¾ cup powdered sugar
1½ cups flour
Pinch salt
⅓ cup cocoa
Walnuts, halved
Maraschino cherries

Preheat oven to 300 degrees. Cream butter and powdered sugar until fluffy. Stir in flour, salt, and cocoa. Mix well. If too soft, chill in refrigerator for ½ hour. Shape into 1-inch balls and place on an ungreased cookie sheet about 2 inches apart. Flatten balls with a fork. Top with a walnut half or a cherry. Bake for 20 to 25 minutes. Remove from oven and let cool slightly before removing from pan.

Day 50

Chocolate Popcorn Balls
. . . .

3 cups popping corn
1½ cups molasses
1 cup sugar
1 tablespoon baking soda
1 cup mini chocolate chips

Pop 3 batches of popping corn. Place in large pan.
In a saucepan, bring molasses and sugar to a boil.
While boiling, stir in baking soda. Pour over
popcorn and mix. Allow to cool completely.
Add chocolate chips to cooled mixture.
Slightly grease hands and shape into balls.
Wrap in waxed paper.

Day 51

Chocolate Peanut Butter Cups

. . . .

1 (12 ounce) package milk
chocolate chips, divided
1 cup peanut butter
½ cup powdered sugar

*Trim 12 paper muffin cup liners to half their
height. In microwavable bowl, microwave half
the chocolate chips for 2 minutes, stirring after
each minute. Spoon melted chocolate into muffin
cups, filling halfway. With spoon, spread
chocolate up sides of cups until evenly coated.
Cool in refrigerator until firm. In small bowl,
mix together peanut butter and powdered
sugar. Divide evenly into chocolate cups.
Melt remaining chocolate and spoon over
peanut butter. Spread chocolate to edges of cups.*

Day 52

Chocolate Almond Pie
. . . .

½ cup milk
16 large marshmallows
6 chocolate-almond candy bars
1 cup whipping cream, whipped
1 (9 inch) piecrust, baked and cooled
Sweetened whipped cream
Chocolate curls

Heat milk in saucepan until hot; dissolve marshmallows in hot milk. Break and add candy bars. Stir until melted. Remove from heat and cool. Fold in 1 cup whipped cream. Pour into baked 9-inch piecrust. Refrigerate until set. Serve with sweetened whipped cream and chocolate curls.

Day 53

Wacky Cake
. . . .

3 cups flour
2 cups sugar
2 teaspoons baking soda
½ cup cocoa, plus extra for dusting pan
1 teaspoon salt
⅔ cup vegetable oil
2 teaspoons vanilla
2 tablespoons vinegar
2 cups warm water

Preheat oven to 350 degrees. Grease 9x13-inch pan and dust with cocoa. In a large bowl, sift together flour, sugar, baking soda, cocoa, and salt. Make 3 wells. In first well, pour oil and vanilla. In second well, pour vinegar. In third well, pour water. Mix well. Pour into prepared pan. Bake for 30 minutes.

Day 54

Slow Cooker Cherry Chocolate Dessert
• • • • • • • • • • • • • • •

1 (21 ounce) can cherry pie filling
1 (18 ounce) package chocolate fudge cake mix
½ cup butter

*Place pie filling in slow cooker.
Combine dry cake mix and butter. Sprinkle over
filling. Cover and cook on low for 3 hours.*

Day 55

Chocolate Date Pudding

4 cups brown sugar, divided
3½ cups water
2 tablespoons butter
1 cup chopped dates
½ cup semisweet chocolate chips
1 cup chopped nuts
1 cup sweetened condensed milk
2 cups flour, sifted
4 teaspoons baking powder

*Preheat oven to 350 degrees. In saucepan,
bring 3 cups brown sugar, water, and butter to a
boil to create syrup. In separate bowl, mix 1 cup
brown sugar with dates, chocolate chips, nuts,
condensed milk, flour, and baking powder. Pour
syrup into bottom of greased 9x13-inch pan.
Drop dough by spoonfuls into syrup.
Bake for 45 to 60 minutes.*

Day 56

Popcorn Cake
· · · · · · · · · · · · ·

4 quarts popped popcorn
½ cup candy-coated chocolate pieces
1 cup chopped nuts
1½ pounds mini marshmallows
¼ cup vegetable oil
½ cup butter

*Combine popcorn, candy-coated chocolate pieces,
and nuts in large bowl; mix well. In saucepan,
combine marshmallows, oil, and butter.
Cook until marshmallows and butter are melted,
stirring constantly. Pour over popcorn mixture.
Pat into greased Bundt pan. Turn upside
down onto plate until cake releases.*

Day 57

White Hot Chocolate
. . . .

3 cups half-and-half, divided
⅔ cup vanilla baking chips
1 cinnamon stick
⅛ teaspoon ground nutmeg
1 teaspoon vanilla
¼ teaspoon almond extract
Ground cinnamon (optional)

*Place ¼ cup half-and-half, vanilla chips,
cinnamon stick, and nutmeg in saucepan; stir
over low heat until chips are melted. Discard
cinnamon stick. Add remaining half-and-half.
Stir until thoroughly heated. Remove from heat,
then add vanilla and almond extract. Pour into
four mugs. Garnish with cinnamon if desired.*

Day 58

Chocolate Cream Pie
. . . .

1¾ cups cold milk
2 small boxes instant chocolate pudding
1 (8 ounce) container frozen
whipped topping, thawed
1 prepared 9-inch graham cracker crust

Pour cold milk into large mixing bowl.
Add pudding mix. Beat with whisk until well
mixed. Gently stir in whipped topping. Spoon
into crust. Refrigerate for 4 hours or until set.

Day 59

Endless Possibilities
. . . .

A great gift for the chocolate lover is a
basket filled with chocolaty treats: a variety
of candy bars, brownies with fudge icing, truffles,
a german-chocolate cake mix, fudge, chocolate
syrup, an instant chocolate pudding mix,
chocolate-covered pretzels, a hot cocoa mix. . .
The possibilities are endless!

FROM *STIRRIN' UP CHOCOLATE & JOY*

Day 60

White Chocolate Pie
. . . .

1 (12 ounce) package white chocolate chips
½ cup whipping cream
¼ cup butter
2 teaspoons light corn syrup
1 (10 ounce) bag frozen raspberries, thawed
1 10-inch baked pie shell

Microwave chips until melted. In saucepan, combine whipping cream, butter, and corn syrup. Bring to a boil, stirring constantly. Pour over chocolate; stir until blended and smooth. Stir in raspberries. Spoon into pie shell. Chill until firm.

Day 61

Snickerdoodle Cake
. . . .

1 German chocolate cake mix
1 (14 ounce) package caramels
½ cup margarine
⅓ cup milk
¾ cup semisweet chocolate chips
1 cup walnuts, chopped

*Prepare cake mix according to package directions.
Pour half of batter into greased 9x13-inch baking
pan. Bake at 350 degrees for 20 minutes. Melt
caramels with margarine and milk in saucepan
over low heat, stirring frequently. Pour over
baked cake. Sprinkle with chocolate chips and
nuts. Spoon remaining cake batter over caramel
layer. Bake at 250 degrees for 20 minutes.
Increase temperature to 350 degrees and
bake for an additional 10 minutes.*

Day 62

Frozen Chips Tip
. . . .

To help your chocolate chips maintain their
shape in your desserts, freeze the chocolate chips
before adding them to your ready-to-bake
cookie dough or cake batter.

FROM *STIRRIN' UP CHOCOLATE & JOY*

Day 63

Slow Cooker Triple Chocolate Delight
. . . .

1 (18 ounce) package chocolate fudge cake mix
1 pint sour cream
1 (4 ounce) box instant chocolate pudding mix
1 (12 ounce) package milk chocolate chips
¾ cup oil
4 eggs
1 cup water

Spray slow cooker with nonstick spray.
Mix all ingredients. Pour into slow cooker.
Cook on low for 4 to 5 hours.
Serve warm with ice cream.

Day 64

Chicken with Chocolate Sauce

. . . .

1½ pounds boneless
   chicken breasts,
   cut into strips
Pepper to taste
Cinnamon to taste
2 bay leaves

1 teaspoon thyme
1 clove garlic, chopped
1 cup vegetable oil
1 onion, chopped
2 tablespoons cocoa

In plastic bag, combine chicken strips, spices, garlic, and oil. Refrigerate for about 1 hour or until well marinated. Heat 2 tablespoons marinade in saucepan. Add remaining chicken strips and brown. Add onion and marinade to saucepan and continue cooking over low heat. Cook for 20 minutes; then stir in cocoa. Cook for 10 more minutes. Remove chicken with slotted spoon. Reduce sauce and serve over chicken.

Day 65

Banana Bread
· · · · · · · · · · ·

1 cup sugar
½ cup butter, softened
2 eggs, beaten
3 ripe bananas, mashed
2 cups flour, sifted
1 teaspoon baking soda
1 cup semisweet chocolate chips
½ cup chopped nuts

Preheat oven to 350 degrees.
Combine all ingredients in order listed.
Bake in greased loaf pan for 1 hour.

Day 66

Mocha Balls
· · · · · · · · · ·

1 cup butter, softened
½ cup sugar
2 teaspoons vanilla
2 teaspoons instant coffee powder
¼ cup cocoa
1¾ cups flour
2 cups finely chopped pecans
Powdered sugar

Preheat oven to 325 degrees. In large bowl, cream butter, sugar, and vanilla until light. Add coffee powder, cocoa, and flour. Mix well. Add pecans. Shape into 1-inch balls and place on ungreased cookie sheets. Bake for 17 to 20 minutes. Roll in powdered sugar while warm.

Day 67

White Chocolate Cherry Lemon Cookies
. . . .

1 box lemon cake mix
2 eggs
1 cup dried cherries
½ cup vegetable oil
1 cup white chocolate chips

*Preheat oven to 350 degrees. Combine
all ingredients in bowl and mix well with spoon.
Drop by heaping tablespoons onto ungreased
cookie sheet. Bake for 8 to 10 minutes. Do not
overbake. Remove to wire rack to cool.*

Day 68

Kristy's Chocolate Cookie Truffles
. . . .

1 (16 ounce) package chocolate
sandwich cookies, divided
1 (8 ounce) package cream cheese, softened
4 ounces semisweet chocolate chips, melted
4 ounces milk chocolate chips, melted

*Crush 9 of the cookies to fine crumbs and reserve
for later. Crush remaining cookies and place in
bowl. Add cream cheese; mix until well blended.
Roll mixture into balls. Coat with chocolate.
Sprinkle with reserved cookie crumbs.*

Day 69

Marble Bars
. . . .

½ cup peanut butter
⅓ cup butter
¾ cup sugar
¾ cup brown sugar
2 eggs
1 cup flour
1 teaspoon baking powder
¼ teaspoon salt
2 teaspoons vanilla
2 cups semisweet chocolate chips

Preheat oven to 350 degrees. Cream peanut butter, butter, and sugars; add eggs. Add dry ingredients and vanilla, mixing well. Spread in greased 9x13-inch pan. Sprinkle chips over top. Bake for 5 minutes. Swirl chips through batter to create marble effect. Return to oven and bake for 25 minutes or until lightly browned.

Day 70

White Chocolate Pretzels
. . . .

1 cup white chocolate chips
1 bag pretzel twists
Sprinkles (optional)

*In double boiler over low heat, melt white
chocolate chips, stirring until smooth. Dip
pretzels in chocolate until completely coated.
Remove using pair of tongs. Place on waxed
paper to cool. Decorate with sprinkles if desired.*

Day 71

Chocolate Coffee Beans
. . . .

¼ cup dark roasted coffee beans, whole
½ cup milk chocolate chips

Break whole coffee beans in half along ridge on bean. In small saucepan over low heat, melt chocolate chips, stirring until smooth. Drop coffee bean halves into chocolate by handfuls. Stir beans into chocolate and scoop out with a slotted spoon. Place on waxed paper–lined cookie sheet. Separate so they do not clump together.

Day 72

Dipped Strawberries
. . . .

1 pound fresh strawberries with leaves
2 cups milk chocolate chips
2 tablespoons butter

*Insert toothpicks into tops of strawberries.
In double boiler, melt chocolate chips and butter,
stirring occasionally until smooth. Holding by
toothpicks, dip strawberries into chocolate
mixture. Place on waxed paper to cool.*

Day 73

Dipped Bananas
. . . .

4 bananas
1 (12 ounce) package semisweet
chocolate chips, melted
1 cup finely chopped nuts

*Cut bananas into 2-inch pieces. Using fork,
dip pieces in melted chocolate. Sprinkle with
chopped nuts. Place on waxed paper–lined cookie
sheet and freeze. When frozen, place in
freezer bags. Serve frozen.*

Day 74

Lovely Memories
. . . .

Kitchens aren't just for creating palate-pleasing
meals.... Maybe even more important are some
of the loveliest memories, which are created there.

FROM *IN THE KITCHEN WITH MARY & MARTHA*

Day 75

Chocolate Fruit Balls
. . . .

½ cup chopped dried apricots
⅓ cup chopped raisins
¼ cup grated dark chocolate
¾ cup dark chocolate
¼ cup butter

*In small bowl, combine apricots, raisins,
and grated dark chocolate. Roll teaspoons of
mixture into balls and refrigerate overnight.
Break chocolate into pieces and place in top of
double boiler with butter over simmering water.
Stir until smooth. Dip each fruit ball in chocolate
until evenly coated. Place balls on foil-covered
trays; allow to set in a cool place.*

Day 76

Peppermint Patty Cocoa
· ·

10 chocolate sandwich cookies, coarsely chopped
3 cups milk
½ cup chocolate syrup
½ teaspoon peppermint extract

*Place all ingredients in blender; cover.
Blend on high speed until well blended. Pour into
2-quart saucepan. Cook on medium-high heat
until heated through, stirring frequently.
Pour into coffee mugs.*

Day 77

Chocolate Orange Truffles
. . . .

1 package chocolate sandwich cookies
4 ounces milk chocolate chips
1 (8 ounce) package cream cheese, softened
1 teaspoon orange extract
1 teaspoon orange peel
8 ounces dark chocolate candy coating, melted

Crush cookies in a resealable plastic bag.
Melt chocolate and stir in cream cheese,
extract, and orange peel until smooth.
Stir in cookie crumbs. Form into balls,
cool, and then coat with chocolate.

Day 78

White Chocolate Coffee
. . . .

⅓ cup white chocolate chips
2 cups half-and-half
2 cups hot fresh-brewed coffee
Whipped topping

In medium microwavable bowl, microwave chocolate chips and half-and-half on high for 2 minutes, stirring halfway through cooking time. Stir until chocolate is completely melted and mixture is smooth. Stir in coffee. Pour into large cups or mugs. Top each serving with whipped topping. Serve immediately.

Day 79

White Chocolate Graham Crackers
. . . .
1 box graham crackers
1 (12 ounce) package white chocolate chips
Sprinkles

*Break graham crackers in half. In small
saucepan over low heat, melt white chocolate
chips stirring until smooth. Dip halved graham
crackers into chocolate to coat completely.
Place on waxed paper. Before graham
crackers cool, decorate with sprinkles.*

Day 80

Dipped Stuffed Dates
. . . .

1 small box whole dates
Walnut halves
1 cup semisweet chocolate chips

*Stuff each date with walnut half.
In small saucepan over medium heat, melt
chocolate, stirring until smooth. Drop dates in
chocolate and roll until completely coated. Place on
waxed paper–lined cookie sheet to cool.*

Dipped Peanut Brittle
• • • • • • • • • • • • • • • •

1 cup sugar
½ cup light corn syrup
1 cup peanuts
1 teaspoon butter
1 teaspoon vanilla
1 teaspoon baking soda
1½ cups milk chocolate chips

*In microwavable bowl, combine sugar
and corn syrup. Microwave on high for
4 minutes, stirring once every minute. Add
peanuts; microwave for 3½ minutes. Add butter
and vanilla; microwave an additional 1½
minutes. Add baking soda and stir gently
until mixture is foamy. Pour out onto
greased jelly-roll pan to cool. Break into
pieces. Melt chocolate chips. Dip brittle in
melted chocolate to completely coat.
Place on waxed paper to cool.*

Day 82

Chocolate Chai
. . . .

1 bag black tea
½ cup boiling water
3 tablespoons sugar
2 tablespoons cocoa
2 cups milk
1 teaspoon vanilla
½ teaspoon nutmeg
Whipped topping

*In small saucepan, pour boiling water over
tea bag. Cover and let stand for 3 to 5 minutes.
Remove tea bag. Stir in sugar and cocoa. Cook
and stir over medium heat just until mixture
comes to a boil. Stir in milk, vanilla, and nutmeg;
heat thoroughly. Do not boil. Pour into cups.
Top with whipped topping.*

Day 83

Mocha Spiced Coffee
. . . .

1½ teaspoons cinnamon
½ teaspoon nutmeg
5 cups fresh-brewed coffee
1 cup milk
¼ cup packed brown sugar
⅓ cup chocolate syrup
1 teaspoon vanilla

Mix cinnamon and nutmeg in with coffee grounds to make 5 cups coffee. Make coffee in coffeemaker. In heavy saucepan, combine milk, brown sugar, and chocolate syrup. Cook over low heat, stirring frequently and making sure milk does not boil. Once sugar is dissolved, add vanilla and brewed coffee.

Day 84

Chocolate Delight
. . . .

1 small box chocolate instant pudding
2 cups milk
2 cups frozen whipped topping, thawed, divided
Garnish (chocolate chips, grated chocolate,
chocolate cookie crumbs, or strawberries)

*Prepare pudding with milk as directed
on package. Fold 1½ cups whipped topping
into pudding; spoon into four dessert dishes.
Top with remaining ½ cup whipped topping
and chocolate or strawberry garnish.*

Day 85

Chocolate Banana Fizz
. . . .

1 cup fat-free frozen vanilla yogurt
⅛ cup fat-free hot fudge syrup
1 banana, sliced
½ cup club soda

Place all ingredients in blender.
Cover and blend on high speed
until smooth. Serve immediately.

Day 86

Chocolate Caramel Pecan Smoothie
· ·

1 pint frozen chocolate yogurt
⅓ cup caramel ice-cream topping
2 tablespoons chopped pecans
¾ cup milk

Place all ingredients in blender. Cover and blend on medium speed for 30 to 40 seconds or until smooth. Pour into 2 serving glasses.

Day 87

Chocolate Punch
. . . .

¾ cup semisweet chocolate chips
2 cups hot water
½ cup sugar
2 quarts milk
2 teaspoons vanilla
1 quart vanilla ice cream
1 quart club soda

In small saucepan, melt chocolate chips over low heat. In large saucepan, add melted chocolate to water along with sugar. Heat chocolate mixture until just boiling, stirring constantly. Add milk and cook until heated through. Stir in vanilla. Chill; then pour chocolate mixture into punch bowl over ice cream. Add club soda.

Day 88

Chocolate Yogurt Refresher
. . . .

1 (8 ounce) cup strawberry yogurt
1 cup chilled milk
½ cup sliced strawberries
3 tablespoons chocolate syrup

*Place all ingredients in blender and blend
until smooth. Serve over crushed ice.*

Day 89

Pleasant Hours of Life

· · · · · · · · · · · · · · · · · · · ·

Ponder well on this point: the pleasant hours
of our life are all connected by a more or less
tangible link with some memory of the table.

CHARLES PIERRE MONSELET

Day 90

Chocolate Zucchini Bread
. . . .

2 cups shredded
  zucchini
3 eggs
½ cup applesauce
2 cups sugar
½ cup vegetable oil
3¼ cups flour, sifted

½ cup cocoa
3 teaspoons cinnamon
1 teaspoon baking soda
¼ teaspoon baking
  powder
1 cup semisweet
  chocolate chips

*Preheat oven to 350 degrees. Grease and flour
2 loaf pans. In mixing bowl, mix together
zucchini, eggs, applesauce, sugar, and oil. Add
remaining ingredients. Divide batter between
prepared pans. Bake for 30 to 40 minutes or until
toothpick inserted in center comes out clean.*

Day 91

Dipped Marshmallows
. . . .

3 (12 ounce) packages chocolate chips
1 (14 ounce) can sweetened condensed milk
1 (7 ounce) jar marshmallow crème
1 cup chopped pecans
1 teaspoon vanilla
1½ pounds large marshmallows

*In double boiler over low heat, melt chips.
Add condensed milk, marshmallow crème, pecans,
and vanilla. Into warm mixture, dip individual
large marshmallows. Dry on waxed paper.
Place in refrigerator to set if desired.*

Day 92

Dipped Peanuts
. . . .

¾ cup semisweet chocolate chips
¼ cup light corn syrup
1 tablespoon water
2 cups unsalted peanuts

*Combine chocolate chips, corn syrup,
and water in top of double boiler over hot water.
Stir until melted. Remove from heat and
add peanuts, stirring until well coated.
Place on waxed paper to cool.*

Day 93

Do Not Worry. . .
. . . .

*"Therefore I tell you, do not worry about your life,
what you will eat or drink."*

MATTHEW 6:25

Day 94

Chewy Sticks
. . . .

2 (12 ounce) packages semisweet chocolate chips
1 (12 ounce) package licorice sticks, any flavor

*In double boiler over low heat,
melt chocolate chips until smooth. Dip licorice
sticks about three-quarters into chocolate. Hold
above pan to let excess drip off. Place on cookie
sheet lined with waxed paper until cool.*

Day 95

Chunky Chocolate Peanut Butter Balls
· · · · · · · · · · · · · · · ·

½ cup butter
1 cup chunky peanut butter
2 cups powdered sugar
3 cups crispy rice cereal
Dark chocolate candy coating

*Melt butters in a pan and add sugar,
stirring often. Remove from heat and stir in
cereal. Form into balls and cool in refrigerator
for 1 hour. Melt chocolate in microwave
and coat with chocolate.*

Day 96

Easy Microwave Truffles
· · · · · · · · · · · · · · · · · · · ·

8 ounces semisweet chocolate
¼ cup butter
¼ cup whipping cream
¼ teaspoon almond extract
⅓ cup finely chopped pecans, toasted, divided

*In a microwavable bowl, combine chocolate
and butter. Microwave until melted. Stir in
cream and extract. Beat until slightly thickened,
scraping sides of bowl. Immediately pour
into prepared cups. Roll in pecans.
Refrigerate until set.*

Day 97

Snack Mix
· · · · · · · · ·

2 cups bear-shaped chocolate graham snacks
4 cups popped popcorn
2 cups mini chocolate sandwich cookies
2 cups candy-coated chocolate pieces
1 cup Gummy Bears

Mix all ingredients in large bowl.
Separate into snack-size plastic bags.

Day 98

Chocolate Berry Bonbons
. . . .

1 cup milk chocolate chips
1 (8 ounce) package cream cheese, softened
2 tablespoons strawberry preserves
1 (12 ounce) box vanilla wafers
8 ounces milk chocolate candy coating, melted

*Melt chocolate chips and stir in cream cheese
and preserves. Crush cookies and add to
chocolate mixture. Shape into small balls,
cool, then coat with chocolate.*

Day 99

Chocolate Peanut Delights
. . . .
2 cups milk chocolate candy coating
2 cups dry-roasted peanuts

Melt chocolate and stir in peanuts.
Drop by spoonful onto waxed paper
and let set up in refrigerator.

Day 100

Chocolate Marshmallow Delights
. . . .

2 cups milk chocolate candy coating
2 cups mini marshmallows

Melt chocolate and stir in marshmallows.
Drop by spoonful onto waxed paper
and let set up in refrigerator.

Day 101

Tasty Turtles
· · · · · · · · · · · ·

3 cups milk chocolate candy coating
1 cup pecans
1 cup caramel baking balls
1 cup coconut

Melt chocolate and stir in other ingredients.
Drop by spoonful onto waxed paper
and let set up in refrigerator.

Day 102

Applesauce Bread
. . . .

1 cup butter, softened	2 cups applesauce
3 cups sugar	3 cups flour
4 egg whites, whipped	¾ cup cocoa, sifted
1 tablespoon vanilla	1 teaspoon baking soda
1 teaspoon almond extract	½ teaspoon baking powder

Preheat oven to 325 degrees. In mixing bowl, combine butter, sugar, egg whites, vanilla, almond extract, and applesauce. In another mixing bowl, combine flour, cocoa, baking soda, and baking powder. Mix wet ingredients with dry ingredients just until moistened. Pour batter into 2 greased loaf pans and bake for 40 minutes.

Day 103

Chocolate Peanut Butter Crackers

. . . .

2 cups milk chocolate candy coating
1 box mini crackers with peanut butter

Melt chocolate and coat crackers
with it. Place on waxed paper
and let set up in refrigerator.

Day 104

Kristy's Munchies
· · · · · · · · · · · · · · ·

2 cups almonds, roasted and salted
1 cup chocolate-covered raisins

*Mix together almonds and chocolate-covered
raisins, place in bowl and serve.*

Day 105

Surprise!
. . . .

Share some love from your kitchen.
Surprise your coworkers with a chocolaty treat.

Day 106

Quick Chocolate Drops
· · · · · · · · · · · · · · · · · · · ·

3 cups quick oats
1 cup flaked coconut
6 tablespoons cocoa
½ cup butter
½ cup milk
2 cups sugar
½ teaspoon vanilla

*Mix oats, coconut, and cocoa. In saucepan,
combine butter, milk, sugar, and vanilla; heat
until almost boiling (but do not boil). Pour over
dry mixture and stir well. Drop by spoonfuls
onto buttered waxed paper. Chill until firm.*

Day 107

Peachy Bonbons
. . . .

1 cup white chocolate chips
1 (8 ounce) package cream cheese, softened
2 tablespoons peach preserves
1 (12 ounce) box vanilla wafers
8 ounces white chocolate
candy coating, melted

*Melt chocolate chips and stir in cream cheese
and preserves. Crush cookies and add to
chocolate mixture. Shape into small balls,
cool, then coat with chocolate.*

Day 108

Chocolate Hay Stacks
. . . .

1 (12 ounce) package
semisweet chocolate chips
2 cups coconut
2 cups chinese noodles

Melt chocolate and stir in other ingredients.
Drop by spoonful onto waxed paper,
and let set up in refrigerator.

Day 109

Chocolate Cupcake Trifle

. . . .

2 (14 ounce) packages
prepared chocolate pudding
1 (8 ounce) package cream cheese, softened
1 (12 ounce) container frozen
whipped topping, thawed, divided
24 frosted chocolate cupcakes
1 (8 ounce) package peanut butter cups

*In large bowl, combine the pudding with the
cream cheese. Fold in ½ cup of the whipped
topping and set aside. Crumble one-third of
the cupcakes into a large glass bowl. Top with
one-third of the pudding mixture and one-third
of the remaining whipped topping. Sprinkle
with peanut butter cups. Repeat layers,
ending with candy. Cover and refrigerate
for several hours before serving.*

Day 110

Thin Chocolate Chip Cookies
. . . .

1½ cups sugar
1 cup margarine
2 eggs
2 teaspoons vanilla
2½ cups Grape-Nuts Flakes cereal
1 cup semisweet chocolate chips
2 cups flour
1 teaspoon baking soda
⅛ teaspoon salt

*Cream sugar and margarine. Add eggs and stir;
add vanilla and stir; add cereal and chocolate
chips and stir. In separate bowl, combine flour,
baking soda, and salt then add gradually to cereal
mixture. Stir well. Drop by teaspoonfuls onto
ungreased cookie sheets and bake at 350 degrees
for 20 minutes or until golden brown. (Bake for
a less amount of time for smaller cookies.)*

Day 111

Mini White Chocolate–Covered Pretzels
· · · · · · · · · · · · · · · · · · · ·

6 (1 ounce) squares white chocolate
1 (15 ounce) package mini twist pretzels
¼ cup colored candy sprinkles (optional)

*Melt white chocolate in top of double boiler,
stirring constantly. Dip pretzel halfway into
white chocolate, completely covering half of
pretzel. Roll in topping if desired and lay
on waxed paper. Continue process until no
white chocolate remains. Place pretzels in
refrigerator for 15 minutes to harden.
Store in airtight container.*

Day 112

Quick Chocolate Truffles
. . . .

4 cups milk chocolate chips
1 (8 ounce) container whipped topping
1¼ cups graham cracker crumbs

Microwave chocolate chips on medium-high heat for 1 minute. Stir; microwave 10 to 20 seconds longer or until chips are melted. Cool for about 30 minutes, stirring occasionally. Fold in whipped topping. Drop by rounded teaspoonfuls onto waxed paper–lined cookie sheets. Freeze until firm, about 1½ hours. Shape into balls and roll in graham cracker crumbs. Refrigerate in airtight containers. If desired, truffles may be frozen and then removed from freezer 30 minutes before serving.

Day 113

Rocky Road Candy
. . . .

2 cups (1 bag) semisweet chocolate chips
½ bag colored miniature marshmallows
⅓ cup pecans, chopped

*Melt chocolate over low heat, or use double boiler
or microwave. Stir in marshmallows and
pecans. Spoon onto waxed paper. Form into log.
Refrigerate for 2 hours. Slice into ½-inch pieces.*

Day 114

Rocky Road Ice-Cream Sandwiches

1 cup canned chocolate fudge frosting
½ cup mini marshmallows
32 graham cracker squares
1 cup marshmallow crème
½ gallon chocolate ice cream, softened

Mix frosting and mini marshmallows together gently. Spread half of graham crackers with this frosting mixture. Spread the other half of graham crackers with marshmallow crème. Make sandwiches with the two graham crackers placing ½ cup of chocolate ice cream in the middle. Press together gently, then wrap individually in plastic wrap and freeze until firm.

Day 115

Decadent Brownie Pie
· · · · · · · · · · · · · · · · · ·

1 cup milk chocolate chips
1 (9 inch) piecrust
1 (15 ounce) package brownie mix
⅓ cup water
1 egg
1 ounce square semisweet chocolate, melted

*Sprinkle chocolate chips over the bottom of
piecrust. Beat together brownie mix, water, egg,
and melted chocolate in a medium bowl. Pour
over chips in pie pan. Bake at 375 degrees for
35 minutes until crust is golden brown.
Allow to cool for one hour before serving.
Serve with vanilla ice cream.*

Day 116

Chocolate Drop Cookies
. . . .

½ cup shortening
2 squares unsweetened baking chocolate
2 eggs
1 cup sugar
½ teaspoon vanilla
1⅓ cups flour

Preheat oven to 400 degrees. Melt shortening and chocolate together in medium saucepan. Remove from heat. Beat eggs; add sugar and whisk together well. Add melted chocolate mixture, vanilla, and flour. Mix well. Drop by heaping tablespoons onto ungreased cookie sheet. Bake for 6 minutes.

Day 117

Chocolate Cashew Haystacks

2 cups milk chocolate chips
½ cup semisweet chocolate chips
1 cup chopped cashews
1 cup chow mein noodles

Melt chocolate chips over very low heat in saucepan. Stir in cashews and noodles until coated. Drop by teaspoons onto waxed paper and allow to cool.

Day 118

Lasting Imprints
· · · · · · · · · · · · · ·

A simple kindness, like baking an extra
cake and giving it away to a neighbor, has the
potential to make a big impact. Reaching
out to others with your culinary creations
leaves lasting imprints on hearts.

FROM *In the Kitchen with Mary & Martha*

Day 119

Chocolate Chip Cookie Pie

. . . .

2 eggs
½ cup flour
½ cup sugar
½ cup brown sugar
1 cup butter, melted
1½ cups semisweet chocolate chips
1 cup milk chocolate chips
1 (9 inch) unbaked pie shell

Beat eggs well in large bowl. Add flour and sugars and mix until well blended. Stir in butter and add chips. Pour into unbaked pie shell, and bake at 325 degrees for 55 minutes until golden brown. Let cool completely before cutting.

Day 120

Big Chocolate Chip Cookies

. . . .

1 cup margarine
1 cup brown sugar
1 egg
1 teaspoon vanilla
2 cups flour
1 teaspoon baking soda

½ teaspoon salt
1 cup rolled oats
2 cups chocolate chips
½ cup nuts (optional)
½ cup raisins (optional)

Combine margarine, brown sugar, egg, and vanilla. Add flour, baking soda, and salt. Add oats, chocolate chips, and, if desired, nuts and raisins; mix well. Measure ¼ cup dough for each cookie, making each cookie 3 inches in diameter and ½ inch thick. Bake on lightly greased cookie sheets for 15 minutes. Let cool for 5 minutes before removing from sheets.

Day 121

Chocolate Chip Cheesecake
. . . .

1½ cups chocolate sandwich cookie crumbs
3 tablespoons butter, melted
3 (3 ounce) packages cream cheese, softened
1 (14 ounce) can sweetened condensed milk
2 teaspoons vanilla
3 eggs
1 cup semisweet chocolate chips, divided
1 teaspoon flour

*Combine cookie crumbs and butter; press into
9-inch springform pan. Beat cream cheese until
fluffy, then beat in milk, vanilla, and eggs. Toss
½ cup chocolate chips with flour to coat; stir into
cream cheese mixture. Pour into prepared pan
and sprinkle with remaining chips. Bake at 300
degrees for 1 hour or until cake springs back when
lightly touched. Cool. Chill. Serve.*

Day 122

White Chocolate Squares

. . . .

2 cups white chocolate chips, divided
¼ cup butter or margarine
1 cup flour
½ teaspoon baking powder

1 (14 ounce) can sweetened condensed milk
1 cup pecans or walnuts, chopped
1 large egg
1 teaspoon vanilla
Powdered sugar

Grease 9x13-inch baking pan. In large saucepan over low heat, melt 1 cup chips and butter. Stir in flour and baking powder until blended. Stir in sweetened condensed milk, nuts, egg, vanilla, and remaining chips. Spoon mixture into prepared pan. Bake at 350 for 20 to 25 minutes. Cool. Sprinkle with powdered sugar; cut into squares. Store covered at room temperature.

Day 123

Black Forest Trifle
. . . .

1 chocolate fudge cake mix
1 (5.9 ounce) box chocolate instant pudding
1 quart cherry pie filling
3 cups whipping cream, whipped
Chocolate curls
Maraschino cherries

*Prepare cake mix according to package directions
and bake in two layers; slice layers into chunks
after cake cools. Prepare chocolate pudding
according to package directions. In large bowl,
layer chunks of chocolate cake, pudding, pie filling,
and whipped cream—making three repetitions
and ending with layer of cake and cream.
Garnish with whipped cream, chocolate
curls, and cherries. Chill and serve.*

Day 124

A Dust of Cocoa
. . . .

If you prepare your pan with flour when baking
a chocolate dessert, you could end up with an
unsightly white residue on your cake. Instead,
try dusting pans with cocoa instead.

FROM *IN THE KITCHEN WITH MARY & MARTHA*

Day 125

White Chocolate Haystacks
. . . .

2½ cups white chocolate chips
1 cup chopped pecans
1 cup chow mein noodles

*Melt chocolate chips over very low heat
in saucepan. Stir in pecans and noodles
until coated. Drop by teaspoons onto
waxed paper and allow to cool.*

Day 126

Triple Chocolate Chip Cookies
. . . .

1 chocolate cake mix
1 cup sour cream
1 small box instant chocolate pudding
1 cup semisweet chocolate chips
2 large eggs

Combine all five ingredients in bowl.
Stir until moistened and no large lumps remain.
Drop by rounded spoonfuls about 2 inches
apart onto greased cookie sheets.
Bake at 350 degrees for 16 to 18 minutes.
Let stand for 2 minutes. Cool completely.

Day 127

Traditional No-Bake Cookies
. . . .

½ cup butter or margarine
½ cup milk
2 cups sugar
½ cup cocoa
1 cup peanut butter
1 teaspoon vanilla
3 cups oats

Combine butter, milk, sugar, and cocoa in large saucepan. Bring to a rolling boil. Boil for 3 minutes (do not overboil) and add peanut butter, vanilla, and oats. Drop by heaping teaspoonfuls onto sheets of waxed paper. Let cool until firm. Store in airtight container in cool, dry place.

Day 128

Chocolate Almond Tea Cakes

. . . .

¾ cup margarine or butter, softened
⅓ cup powdered sugar
1 cup flour
½ cup instant cocoa mix
½ cup toasted almonds, diced
Additional powdered sugar

Combine margarine and ⅓ cup powdered sugar.
Stir in flour, cocoa mix, and almonds. (Refrigerate
until firm if dough is too soft to shape.) Heat oven
to 325 degrees. Shape dough into 1-inch balls and
place on ungreased cookie sheets. Bake for about
20 minutes or until set. Dip tops into powdered
sugar while still warm. Let cool and dip again.

Day 129

Chocolate Cream Cheese Pie
. . . .

- 4 ounces cream cheese, softened
- 2 tablespoons sugar
- 1 tablespoon milk
- 1 (8 ounce) container whipped topping
- 1 (3 ounce) package instant chocolate pudding mix
- 1 (3 ounce) box instant cream cheese pudding mix
- 2 cups milk
- 1 (9 inch) chocolate cookie crumb crust

Combine cream cheese, sugar, and 1 tablespoon milk in a large bowl. Beat until smooth. Gently fold in half of the whipped topping. Spread on the bottom of crust. Then combine pudding mixes with 2 cups milk. Beat with wire whisk for 2 minutes. Spread over cream cheese layer. Refrigerate 4 hours or until set. Top with remaining whipped topping.

Day 130

Chocolate Chip Blond Brownies

. . . .

2 cups brown sugar
⅔ cup butter, melted
2 eggs
2 teaspoons vanilla
1 to 2 cups flour
1 teaspoon baking powder
¼ teaspoon baking soda
¼ teaspoon salt
Semisweet chocolate chips

*Add brown sugar to melted butter; cool.
Add eggs and vanilla to mixture and blend
well. In separate bowl, sift flour, baking powder,
baking soda, and salt. Add gradually to sugar
mixture. Pour mixture into greased 8x12-inch
baking pan. Sprinkle chocolate chips on top if
desired. Bake at 350 degrees for 20 to 25 minutes.
(Do not overcook.) Cut into squares.*

Chocolate Chip Coconut Cookies
. . . .

⅓ cup shortening
⅓ cup butter, softened
½ cup sugar
½ cup brown sugar
1 egg
1 teaspoon vanilla
1½ cups flour

½ teaspoon baking soda
½ teaspoon salt
1 cup semisweet
chocolate chips
¼ package flaked
coconut
1 to 2 cups oats

*Mix shortening, butter, sugars, egg,
and vanilla. Blend in flour, baking soda,
and salt. Mix in chocolate chips, coconut, and oats.
Drop by rounded teaspoonfuls 2 inches apart onto
ungreased baking sheets. Bake at 375 degrees
for 8 to 10 minutes. Cool slightly before
removing from baking sheets.*

Day 132

Chewy Chocolate Bars
. . . .

2 cups semisweet chocolate chips
1 (14 ounce) can sweetened condensed milk
¾ cup butter, softened
1¼ cups brown sugar, packed
2 eggs
1½ cups flour
¾ cup rolled oats
½ teaspoon salt

*Melt chocolate chips with milk; set aside.
Cream butter and brown sugar until soft; beat in
eggs. Blend flour, rolled oats, and salt into creamed
mixture. Spread half of batter into greased 9x13-
inch baking pan. Spread chocolate mixture on top
of batter. Spread remaining batter over chocolate
layer. Bake at 350 degrees for 35 minutes.
Cool and cut into bars.*

Day 133

Chocolate Chip
Cream Cheese Cookies
· · · · · · · · · · · · · · · · ·

4 egg yolks
2 cups butter (no substitutions), softened
2 cups sugar
2 (8 ounce) packages cream cheese
2 tablespoons almond extract
4 cups flour
Pinch salt

Combine egg yolks, butter, and sugar. Add cream cheese and almond extract. In separate bowl, combine flour and salt; add to butter mixture. Drop by spoonfuls onto ungreased cookie sheets and bake at 375 degrees until edges turn light brown, approximately 10 minutes.

Day 134

Chocolate Fudge Upside-Down Cake

2 tablespoons shortening
1 cup milk
1 teaspoon salt
2 teaspoons baking powder
1½ cups sugar
2 cups flour
1 teaspoon vanilla
3 tablespoons cocoa

Mix together all cake batter ingredients and spread in 9x13-inch baking pan; sprinkle with nuts if desired. Set aside.

TOPPING:
2 cups sugar
½ cup cocoa
2½ cups boiling water

Mix sugar with cocoa and spread over batter in pan. Then pour boiling water over top. Bake at 375 degrees for 30 minutes.

Day 135

A Happy Kitchen!
. . . .

A messy kitchen is a happy kitchen,
and this kitchen is delirious!

UNKNOWN

Day 136

Chocolate Peanut Butter Squares
• •

1 cup butter, melted
2½ cups peanut butter
5 cups powdered sugar
4 tablespoons butter, melted
1 cup semisweet chocolate chips

*Mix butter and peanut butter until smooth.
Add powdered sugar. Press firmly into 9x13-inch
baking pan. Over low heat, stir melted butter
and chocolate chips until smooth. Spread on top
of peanut butter mixture. Refrigerate
for 2 hours. Cut into squares.*

Day 137

Chocolate Cherry Delicious

· · · · · · · · · · · · · · · · · ·

2 cans cherry pie filling
1 chocolate cake mix
¾ cup butter, melted

*Preheat oven to 350 degrees. Spread pie filling
into 9x13-inch baking pan. Sprinkle dry cake
mix evenly over filling, then drizzle melted butter
over cake mix. (Butter may leave some dry spots
on the dessert.) Bake for 45 minutes or
until done. Serve warm or cold.*

Day 138

Chocolate Eggnog
. . . .

1 (32 ounce) carton chocolate milk
3 cups prepared eggnog
Nutmeg

*Combine chocolate milk and eggnog
in large pitcher or bowl; refrigerate.
Pour into glasses. Sprinkle with nutmeg.*

Day 139

Chocolate Slow Cooker Dessert
. . . .

1 box chocolate cake mix
1 (3 ounce) box instant
vanilla pudding mix
4 eggs
1 cup water
2 cups sour cream
¾ cup vegetable oil
1 cup semisweet chocolate chips

*Spray slow cooker with nonstick cooking spray.
Combine the cake mix and pudding mix in a
large bowl. In a medium bowl, beat the eggs with
the water, then add the sour cream and oil and
beat until smooth. Add to the dry ingredients
and beat well. Stir in the chocolate chips. Pour
into slow cooker. Cover and cook on low for 6 to 8
hours until knife inserted in top comes out clean.*

Day 140

Hot Fudge Pudding

1 cup flour
¼ teaspoon salt
2 tablespoons cocoa
2 teaspoons baking powder
¾ cup sugar
½ cup milk

2 tablespoons shortening
1 cup nuts, chopped
4 tablespoons brown sugar
2 tablespoons cocoa
2 cups hot water

Preheat oven to 350 degrees. Mix flour, salt, cocoa, baking powder, and sugar in bowl. Stir in milk, shortening, and nuts. Spread into 9x9-inch baking pan. Mix brown sugar and 2 tablespoons cocoa and sprinkle over mixture. Pour hot water over top and bake for 40 minutes. Serve with ice cream or whipped topping.

Day 141

S'More Pudding Dessert
. . . .

9 full-size graham crackers, crushed
3¼ cups milk
1 (5 ounce) package (not instant) vanilla pudding
4 (1¼ ounce) chocolate candy bars
2 cups mini marshmallows

*Line bottom of 1½-quart baking dish with
one-third of graham cracker crumbs. Using milk,
cook pudding as directed on package; allow to cool
for 5 minutes. Spread half of pudding over
graham cracker crumbs, then add another third of
cracker crumbs. Place candy bars next, then spread
remaining pudding over chocolate bars. Finish off
layers with remaining third of cracker crumbs;
sprinkle with marshmallows. Broil until
golden brown. Serve warm or chilled.*

Day 142

Chocolate Fondue
. . . .

2 cups heavy cream
3 milk chocolate bars
3 dark or semisweet chocolate bars
1 pound cake cut into cubes
Banana slices, apple slices, strawberries,
marshmallows, vanilla wafers,
and pretzel rods for dipping

In saucepan, heat cream until almost boiling.
Remove from heat and add chocolate in pieces.
Stir mixture until melted. Pour into fondue pot
and serve with fondue forks or bamboo skewers.
Arrange the items to be dipped on a platter.

Day 143

Chunky Chocolate Cookies
. . . .

1 (4 ounce) sweet
  chocolate bar
½ cup butter
½ cup sugar
¼ cup brown sugar
1 egg

1 teaspoon vanilla
1 cup flour
½ teaspoon baking soda
½ teaspoon salt
½ cup nuts, coarsely
  chopped

*Chop chocolate bar into bite-sized pieces;
set aside. Cream butter until soft. Add sugars,
egg, and vanilla; beat until light and fluffy. Add
flour, baking soda, and salt. Stir in chocolate pieces
and nuts. Drop by teaspoonfuls 2 inches apart
onto ungreased cookie sheets. Bake at 375 degrees
for 8 to 10 minutes or until lightly browned.*

Day 144

Chocolate Banana Cream Pie
. . . .

4 ounces cream cheese, softened
2 tablespoons sugar
1 tablespoon milk
1 (8 ounce) container
frozen whipped topping, thawed
2 (3.9 ounce) boxes
instant banana pudding mix
2 cups milk
1 (9 inch) prepared chocolate cookie crumb crust

Combine cream cheese, sugar, and 1 tablespoon milk in a large bowl. Beat until smooth. Gently fold in half of the whipped topping. Spread on the bottom of crust. Then combine pudding mix with 2 cups milk. Beat with wire whisk for 2 minutes. Spread over cream cheese layer. Refrigerate 4 hours or until set. Top with remaining whipped topping.

Day 145

Chocolate Peanut Butter Pie
. . . .

2 cups extra crunchy peanut butter

1 (8 ounce) package fat-free cream cheese, softened

2 cups powdered sugar

1 cup skim milk

3 (8 ounce) containers frozen whipped topping, thawed

3 (9 inch) prepared chocolate crumb piecrusts

Mix peanut butter and cream cheese until smooth. Add powdered sugar, milk, and 12 ounces (1½ containers) whipped topping. Blend thoroughly and pour into piecrusts, spreading evenly. Top each pie with 4 ounces whipped topping. (These pies freeze and keep well.) For added freshness, store pies in 1-gallon freezer bags.

Day 146

Apricots Dipped in Chocolate
. . . .

3 squares white chocolate
3 squares milk chocolate
20 dried apricots

Melt chocolate in microwave. Holding apricots by one end, dip in chocolate halfway. Place on tray or cookie sheet lined with waxed paper. Allow to cool. Arrange apricots on platter and serve.

Day 147

Oven-Shy Cookies
. . . .
1 (16 ounce) package marshmallows
2 cups semisweet chocolate chips
¼ cup butter or margarine
3 cups crispy rice cereal
1 (12 ounce) can salted peanuts

*In saucepan over low heat, cook and stir
marshmallows, chips, and butter until
marshmallows are melted and mixture is smooth.
Remove from heat. Stir in cereal and peanuts;
mix well. Drop by rounded tablespoonfuls
onto waxed paper to cool.*

Day 148

Sweet Revival
· · · · · · · · · · ·

If you are not feeling well, if you
have not slept, chocolate will revive you.

MARQUISE DE SÉVIGNÉ

Day 149

After-Dinner Ice Cream
. . . .

¾ cup whole milk, chilled
⅔ cup sugar
1 cup light cream
½ cup whipping cream
1 teaspoon peppermint extract
1 package after-dinner
chocolate-covered mints

*Using hand mixer or whisk, combine milk
and sugar in bowl. Stir until sugar is dissolved,
1 to 2 minutes. Stir in creams and extract.
Follow ice-cream machine instructions.
Chop after-dinner mints into small pieces.
About 5 minutes before ice cream is done,
add desired amount of mint pieces.*

Day 150

Sugar-Free Chocolate Pudding Pie
• •

1 (3 ounce) box chocolate pudding mix
1 (3 ounce) box cheesecake pudding mix
4 cups milk
1 graham cracker crust

*Prepare puddings as directed on package in
separate bowls. Pour the chocolate pudding mix
into pie shell. Next, pour cheesecake pudding over
chocolate pudding. Cover and refrigerate for
at least one hour before serving. Top with
sugar-free whipped topping if desired.*

Day 151

Chocolate Cherry Trifle
. . . .

1 box chocolate cake mix, prepared
2 (4 ounce) boxes chocolate
instant pudding, prepared
1 can cherry pie filling
2 (8 ounce) containers
frozen whipped topping, thawed

*Cut cake into small squares. Layer cake, pudding,
cherry pie filling, and whipped topping. Repeat.*

Day 152

Chocolate Cream Cheese Frosting
(FROM THE KITCHEN OF BARBARA PINKHAM)
. . . .

5 tablespoons butter
4 ounces cream cheese, softened
¼ cup milk
½ cup cocoa
3 cups powdered sugar
1 teaspoon vanilla
½ teaspoon espresso powder

Beat all ingredients together until smooth.

Day 153

Beef Curry
. . . .

1 pound stew beef, cubed
3 tablespoons vegetable oil
2 tablespoons curry powder
1 square unsweetened chocolate
¼ cup molasses
¼ cup tomato sauce
1 quart orange juice

*Brown stew meat in oil. When meat
is lightly browned, add curry and continue
browning. Add remaining ingredients and
bring to a boil. Simmer for about 1 hour,
continuing to add juice as needed.*

Day 154

Chocolate Butter Cream Frosting

· ·

¼ cup butter, softened
2 (1 ounce) packages
liquid unsweetened chocolate
3 cups powdered sugar
⅓ cup milk
1 teaspoon vanilla

*Cream butter with chocolate. Gradually
blend in sugar alternately with milk and vanilla.*

Day 155

Blessed!
· · · · · · ·

Lord, thank You for my home—and for
my kitchen, where I am able to create tasty
dishes for my family. You have provided me with
so much, and I often forget how blessed I am.
I praise You, Lord. Amen.

FROM IN THE KITCHEN WITH MARY & MARTHA

Day 156

Eric's Malted Milk Ball Chiller
. . . .

⅓ cup malted milk balls, crushed
1 cup ice cream
1½ tablespoons chocolate syrup
½ cup milk

*Place all ingredients in blender and
mix until creamy. Serve immediately.*

Day 157

Cheesecake Cookies
· · · · · · · · · · · · · ·

CRUST:
1 cup flour
⅓ cup sugar
⅓ cup butter

FILLING:
1 (8 ounce) package
cream cheese
¼ cup sugar
1 egg
½ teaspoon vanilla
2 tablespoons milk
1 tablespoon lemon juice

Preheat oven to 350 degrees. Blend flour, sugar, and butter with pastry cutter. Reserve ½ cup of mixture for topping. Press remainder of mixture into 8x8-inch pan. Bake for 12 to 15 minutes. Soften cream cheese with spoon and blend in sugar. Add remaining ingredients and beat well. Spread over crust. Sprinkle with reserved topping. Bake for 25 minutes. Cool and cut into squares. Refrigerate before serving. Drizzle with chocolate syrup.

Day 158

Choco-Cheesecake Freeze

4 ounces cream cheese, softened
2 cups milk, divided
6 scoops chocolate ice cream

*Place cream cheese and 1 cup milk in blender;
blend until smooth. Place remaining milk
and ice cream in blender and continue
to blend until smooth. Serve cold.*

Day 159

Homemade Pudding
. . . .

½ cup sugar
3 tablespoons cornstarch
⅓ cup cocoa
¼ teaspoon salt
2½ cups milk
½ teaspoon vanilla
Mini chocolate chips

In a saucepan, mix sugar, cornstarch, cocoa, and salt. Stir in milk and cook over medium heat, stirring constantly until thick. Stir and cook for 3 more minutes and stir in vanilla. Chill. Top with mini chocolate chips before serving.

Day 160

Chocolate Nutty Layer Pie
. . . .

1 cup flour
½ cup butter, melted
2 tablespoons brown sugar
1 cup chopped walnuts, divided
1 (8 ounce) package cream cheese
1 cup powdered sugar
Whipped topping
1 (4 ounce) box instant
chocolate pudding mix, prepared

*Mix flour, butter, brown sugar, and half of the
walnuts and press in bottom of 9x13-inch pan.
Bake at 350 degrees for 15 minutes. Cool.
Blend cream cheese and powdered sugar. Stir
in 1 cup whipped topping and spread on crust.
Add prepared pudding. Refrigerate until firm.
Spread remaining frozen whipped topping over
pudding layer. Sprinkle with remaining walnuts.*

Day 161

Chocolate Lollipops

Red-colored chocolate candy melts
Green-colored chocolate candy melts
White chocolate candy melts
Lollipop sticks
Christmas-themed lollipop molds

Melt chocolate in double boiler. Pour chocolate into lollipop molds. Tap molds against work surface to force out any air bubbles. Place lollipop sticks in far enough that they won't fall out. Allow lollipops to cool and set. Gently remove lollipops from mold. You can experiment with decorating the lollipops by "painting" contrast chocolate colors into molds before pouring in main color or by placing sprinkles in molds before adding chocolate.

Day 162

White Chocolate Strawberries
. . . .

6 squares white chocolate
6 squares milk chocolate
15 large strawberries with stems on
Finely chopped nuts
Flaked coconut

Melt chocolate in microwave. Holding
strawberries by stems, dip in chocolate. You
can experiment with dipping in one color and
then another. Place strawberries on tray or
cookie sheet lined with waxed paper.
After a few minutes, drizzle with contrast
color of chocolate or sprinkle with finely
chopped nuts or flaked coconut.

Day 163

Iced Frothy Chocolate
. . . .

3 cups milk
1 egg, beaten
⅓ cup semisweet chocolate chips
1 tablespoon sugar
½ teaspoon cinnamon

*In a medium saucepan, warm milk
over medium-low heat until hot but not boiling.
In a small microwave-safe bowl, mix together
egg, chocolate chips, sugar, and cinnamon.
Microwave on high for 20-second intervals,
stirring in between until melted and smooth. Add
chocolate to the milk and whisk together until well
blended. Allow to cool. Pour into blender with
desired amount of ice. Blend until smooth.*

Day 164

Brownie Pudding
• • • • • • • • • • • • •

1 cup flour
1½ cups sugar
2 tablespoons cocoa
2 teaspoons baking
   powder
½ teaspoon salt
½ cup milk

2 tablespoons oil
1 teaspoon vanilla
½ cup chocolate chips
¾ cup nuts, chopped
1 cup brown sugar
¼ cup cocoa
1 cup hot water

In a large bowl, combine flour, white sugar,
2 tablespoons cocoa, baking powder, and salt.
Add milk, oil, and vanilla. Beat until smooth.
Add chocolate chips and nuts. Pour into greased
8x8-inch pan. Mix brown sugar and ¼ cup cocoa;
sprinkle over batter. Pour hot water over all.
Bake at 350 degrees for 45 minutes.

Day 165

Chocolate Cottage Cheese Cookies

. . . .

1½ cups shortening
3½ cups sugar
4 eggs
4 teaspoons vanilla
2 cups cottage cheese
1 cup cocoa powder
2 teaspoons baking
  powder

1 teaspoon salt
1 teaspoon baking
  soda
5½ cups flour
1 cup chopped nuts
  and/or chocolate
  chips
Powdered sugar

*In a large bowl, cream shortening, sugar, eggs,
and vanilla. Add cottage cheese, cocoa powder,
baking powder, salt, and baking soda. Slowly
mix in flour. Fold in nuts and/or chips. Shape
dough into balls and roll in powdered sugar.
Bake at 350 degrees for 10 to 15 minutes.*

Day 166

Magic Cookie Bars
. . . .

½ cup margarine or butter
1½ cups graham cracker crumbs
1 (14 ounce) can sweetened condensed milk
1 (6 ounce) package semisweet chocolate chips
1⅓ cups flaked coconut
1 cup nuts, chopped

In 9x13-inch baking pan, melt margarine in oven. Sprinkle crumbs over margarine, mix together, and press into pan. Pour sweetened condensed milk evenly over crumbs. Top evenly with remaining ingredients. Press down firmly. Bake at 350 degrees (or 325 degrees for glass dish) for 25 to 30 minutes or until lightly browned. Cool thoroughly before cutting.

Day 167

Tranquility
· · · · · · · · ·

In the noise and clatter of my kitchen. . .
I possess God in as great tranquility
as if I were on my knees.

BROTHER LAWRENCE

Day 168

Toffee Bar Cake
. . . .

1 box German chocolate cake mix, prepared
1 can sweetened condensed milk
1 jar caramel ice-cream topping
1 (8 ounce) container whipped topping
5 chocolate toffee candy bars, crushed

*While cake is still hot, poke holes in cake
about 1 inch apart, using handle of wooden spoon.
Pour sweetened condensed milk and ice-cream
topping mixture over cake, making sure cake is
completely covered. Refrigerate overnight. Before
serving, garnish with whipped topping and
sprinkle with toffee candy bar crumbs.*

*Note: Candy bars can be easily crushed by freezing
them first, then breaking them with a hammer.*

Day 169

Chocolate Milk Chiller
. . . .

4 tablespoons chocolate syrup, divided
2 tablespoons raspberry syrup
1 cup chocolate milk

Stir 2 tablespoons chocolate syrup and raspberry syrup into chocolate milk and mix thoroughly. Chill mixture in freezer for 5 minutes. Drizzle remaining chocolate syrup on inside and bottoms of glasses. Pour chilled mixture into chocolate-drizzled glasses.

Day 170

Rebecca's Camping Cream Puffs
. . . .

1 (8 ounce) refrigerated tube crescent rolls
Prepared chocolate pudding cups

*Find a stick that is about 2 inches in diameter
and wrap it in foil. Wrap the crescent rolls around
the stick to form a cone. Cook over the fire until
light brown. Allow to cool. Remove from stick
and spoon pudding into the center. This is fun
to do while camping or in the backyard!*

Day 171

Easy German Chocolate Cake
. . . .

1 box yellow cake mix
½ (3 ounce) box vanilla pudding mix
1 (4 ounce) package Baker's German
sweet chocolate, melted

Prepare cake mix as directed on package.
Add pudding and melted chocolate and mix well.
Bake according to package directions. Top with
icing and broil for 3 minutes. ICING: *Combine ¼*
cup shredded coconut, 1 cup chopped pecans,
1 cup light brown sugar, ½ cup melted butter,
½ cup milk, and 1½ teaspoons vanilla.

Day 172

Giant Chocolate Chip Cookies
• • • • • • • • • • • • • • • • • • • •

2 cups flour
½ teaspoon baking soda
½ teaspoon salt
¾ cup butter
1 cup packed
  brown sugar

½ cup sugar
1 tablespoon vanilla
1 egg, separated
1 (12 ounce) package
  semisweet chocolate
  chips

*Preheat oven to 325 degrees and grease cookie
sheet. Combine dry ingredients and stir with
whisk. Beat butter, sugars, and vanilla. Add
egg white and egg yolk, beating well after each
addition. Add flour mixture and stir until
combined. Stir in chocolate chips. Use ¼ cup
measuring cup to drop cookies onto cookie sheet.
Bake for 13 to 16 minutes.*

Day 173

Chocolate Chip Icebox Cookies
. . . .

1 cup butter, softened
½ cup sugar
½ cup light brown sugar
2 eggs
1½ teaspoons vanilla

¼ teaspoon salt
3 cups flour
¾ cup finely chopped semisweet chocolate chips

Cream butter and sugars; add eggs, vanilla, and salt. Beat until fluffy. Gradually add flour; stir in chocolate chips. Divide dough into 2 logs. Wrap each log in plastic wrap or waxed paper. Refrigerate dough for at least 4 hours or until very firm. Cut into ¼-inch slices and place on greased baking sheet about 1 inch apart. Bake at 350 degrees for 8 to 10 minutes.

Day 174

Chocolate Caramel Mousse
. . . .

1 (7 ounce) package ladyfingers
Caramel ice-cream topping
1 (3 ounce) box instant chocolate pudding mix
1½ cups chocolate milk
4 ounces whipped topping

*Line sides and bottom of 8x8 pan with
ladyfingers. Sprinkle caramel topping lightly over
ladyfingers. Mix pudding mix and chocolate milk.
Cool for 3 to 5 minutes. Fold in whipped
topping and spread over ladyfingers.
Refrigerate until ready to serve.*

Day 175

Chocolate Chip Cream Cheese Drops

. . . .

½ cup butter or
   margarine, softened
3 ounces cream cheese
¼ cup sugar
¼ cup packed
   brown sugar

1 egg
1 teaspoon vanilla
1 cup flour
½ teaspoon salt
1 cup semisweet
   chocolate chips

Preheat oven to 350 degrees. Cream butter, cream cheese, and sugars. Beat in egg and vanilla. Sift together flour and salt; stir into creamed mixture. Stir in chocolate chips. Drop by teaspoons onto lightly greased cookie sheet. Bake for 12 to 15 minutes or until lightly browned around edges. Makes about 3 dozen.

Day 176

Mint Ice-Cream Pie
· · · · · · · · · · · · · · · · ·

½ gallon vanilla ice cream
6 peppermint candies
1 prepared graham cracker crust
Chocolate syrup

*Scoop ice cream into medium bowl. Crush candies
and add to ice cream; stir well. Spoon into crust
and spread evenly. Cover and freeze until
well set, at least 4 hours. Cut into slices.
Drizzle with chocolate syrup.*

Creamy Chocolate
Chip Pudding Cookies
· · · · · · · · · · · · · · · · · ·

2¼ cups flour
1 teaspoon baking soda
1 cup butter, softened
¼ cup sugar
¾ cup packed
   brown sugar

1 small box chocolate or
   vanilla instant pudding
   mix
1 teaspoon vanilla
2 eggs
1 (12 ounce) package
   chocolate chips

*Preheat oven to 375 degrees. Mix flour with
baking soda. Combine butter, sugars, pudding
mix, and vanilla. Beat until smooth. Beat in eggs.
Gradually add flour mixture; stir in chocolate
chips. Drop by rounded teaspoons onto ungreased
cookie sheet. Bake for 8 to 10 minutes.
Makes approximately 5 dozen.*

Day 178

Old English Cookies
. . . .

1 cup shortening
2 cups brown sugar
3 eggs
4 cups flour
1 teaspoon baking soda
1 teaspoon baking powder
½ teaspoon salt

½ teaspoon cinnamon
½ teaspoon nutmeg
1 cup brewed cold coffee
½ teaspoon vanilla
1 cup chopped walnuts
1 cup raisins
1 cup semisweet chocolate chips

Cream shortening and brown sugar.
Add eggs one at a time, beating well until light
and fluffy. Add dry ingredients alternately with
coffee. Beat well. Mix in vanilla, walnuts,
raisins, and chocolate chips. Drop cookies
by tablespoons onto greased cookie sheets.
Bake at 350 for 15 minutes.

Swedish Butter Cookies

• • • • • • • • • • • • • • • • • • • •

2 sticks butter (no substitutions)
1 cup sugar
1 teaspoon vanilla
2 cups flour
1 teaspoon baking powder
Dash salt
Nuts
Candied cherries
Chocolate chips

Preheat oven to 300 degrees. Cream butter and sugar and beat until fluffy. Add vanilla; stir in flour sifted with baking powder and salt. Mix until smooth. Form into small balls; place on ungreased baking sheet. Press nut, cherry, or chocolate chip on top of each. Bake for 20 minutes or until edges are lightly browned.

Day 180

He Is Good
· · · · · · · · ·

Give thanks to the LORD, for he is good.

PSALM 136:1

Day 181

Frozen Banana Pops
. . . .

1 cup semisweet chocolate chips
2 bananas
4 Popsicle sticks
1 cup shredded coconut

*In small saucepan, melt chocolate over low heat.
Cut bananas in half crosswise. Peel bananas
and insert Popsicle stick lengthwise in each.
Roll bananas one at a time in melted chocolate.
Remove from chocolate and roll in shredded
coconut. Place on waxed paper. Freeze for 2 hours.
Save any leftover chocolate for another batch.*

Day 182

Chocolate Oatmeal Raisin Cookies

. . . .

½ cup flour
½ cup wheat flour
½ teaspoon baking
  powder
¼ cup vegetable oil
¼ cup skim milk
½ cup crushed
  pineapple

1 teaspoon lemon juice
1 teaspoon vanilla
1 teaspoon cinnamon
2 cups oatmeal
¾ cup raisins
¼ cup semisweet
  chocolate chips

*Preheat oven to 350 degrees. Mix all ingredients
together. Drop by teaspoons onto ungreased
cookie sheet. Bake for 20 minutes.*

Day 183

Frozen Hot Chocolate
· · · · · · · · · · · · · · · · · · · ·

1 cup 2% milk
1 envelope instant hot chocolate mix
2 tablespoons butter
2 ounces milk chocolate, chopped
2 ounces bittersweet chocolate, chopped
6 ice cubes

Heat milk in saucepan over medium-low heat until bubbles just begin to form around edges and mixture is heated through (approximately 2 minutes). Remove from heat; whisk in hot chocolate mix until well blended. Add butter, milk chocolate, and bittersweet chocolate; stir until smooth. Pour chocolate mixture into blender; add ice. Cover; blend on high speed until well blended. Serve immediately.

Day 184

Banana Chocolate Chip Oatmeal Cookies
. . . .

2 cups mashed bananas
4 cups quick oats
½ teaspoon vanilla
⅔ cup semisweet chocolate chips
½ cup applesauce
½ teaspoon cinnamon

Preheat oven to 350 degrees. Mix all ingredients together until moist. Drop dough by tablespoonfuls on an ungreased cookie sheet. Flatten to desired thickness. Bake for 15 minutes. Store in airtight container.

Day 185

Uplifted Spirits
· · · · · · · · · · · · ·

Invite a friend over for coffee and
a chocolate dessert. You'll find that the
conversation and company will lift your
spirit and rejuvenate your soul.

FROM *IN THE KITCHEN WITH MARY & MARTHA*

Day 186

Triple Chip Wonder Cookies
. . . .

1 box white cake mix
1 stick butter or margarine, melted
2 eggs
½ cup white chocolate chips
½ cup butterscotch chips
½ cup semisweet chocolate chips

*Mix cake mix with melted butter and eggs.
Stir in chips. Drop spoonfuls onto ungreased
cookie sheet. Bake for 6 to 7 minutes
at 350 degrees. Do not overbake;
cookies will set up as they cool.*

Day 187

Trail Mix Cookies

2 medium bananas, mashed
½ cup molasses
¼ cup honey
1 tablespoon cornstarch
½ cup applesauce
¼ cup water
1 teaspoon vanilla

1 cup whole wheat flour
1 teaspoon cinnamon
½ teaspoon baking soda
½ teaspoon cloves
½ cup raisins
½ cup chocolate chips
½ cup peanuts
3 cups quick oats

Mix bananas, molasses, honey, cornstarch, applesauce, water, and vanilla. Stir in flour, cinnamon, baking soda, and cloves. Add remaining ingredients. Form into 16 balls and flatten. Bake at 350 for 12 to 15 minutes on lightly greased cookie sheet.

Day 188

Beef in Chocolate Sauce
. . . .

2 pounds beef tenderloin
Salt and pepper to taste
3 tablespoons vegetable oil
½ finely chopped onion
2 cloves garlic, finely chopped
1 square unsweetened chocolate
2 tablespoons chopped parsley

*Season beef with salt and pepper to taste.
Fry in oil until browned. Add onion and garlic.
Cover and simmer over low heat for about 15
minutes. Add chocolate and simmer uncovered for
10 minutes longer. At serving time, slice meat and
serve with sauce. Sprinkle with parsley.*

Day 189

German Chocolate Cookies
. . . .

1 box German chocolate cake mix
1 stick margarine, softened
2 eggs, beaten
½ cup shredded coconut
24 chocolate-covered soft caramel candies
1 tub chocolate fudge frosting

*Preheat oven to 350 degrees. Mix cake mix,
margarine, eggs, and coconut until well blended.
Pinch off small amount of dough and
form ball. Push caramel candy into center
and roll to reform ball shape. Place on greased
cookie sheet. Bake for 8 to 10 minutes.
Remove from oven and cool. Frost.*

Day 190

Lazy Lemon Cookies
· · · · · · · · · · · · · · · · ·

1 box lemon cake mix
1 stick butter or margarine, melted
2 eggs
2 cups white chocolate chips

*Preheat oven to 350 degrees. Mix cake mix,
butter, and eggs until dough forms. Stir in
chocolate chips. Drop spoonfuls onto ungreased
cookie sheet. Bake for 8 to 10 minutes.
Let cool and store in airtight container.*

Day 191

Chocolate Crinkles
. . . .

1 box chocolate cake mix
1 large egg
¼ cup oil
¼ cup water
1 cup semisweet chocolate chips
2 cups powdered sugar

Preheat oven to 350 degrees. Combine cake mix, egg, oil, and water. Beat until well blended. Stir in chocolate chips. Shape into balls and roll in powdered sugar. Place about 1 inch apart on greased cookie sheet. Bake for 12 to 15 minutes. Sprinkle with additional powdered sugar.

Day 192

Crispy Cake Mix Cookies
. . . .

1 box chocolate cake mix
1 cup crisp rice cereal
½ cup butter, melted
1 egg, slightly beaten
¼ cup semisweet chocolate chips

Preheat oven to 350 degrees. Blend all ingredients. Form into 1-inch balls and place on ungreased cookie sheet. Bake for 9 to 13 minutes.

Day 193

Peanut Butter Chocolate Chip Cake Mix Cookies
. . . .

2 eggs
⅓ cup water
¼ cup butter, softened
1 cup peanut butter
1 box white cake mix
1 (12 ounce) package
semisweet chocolate chips

Preheat oven to 375 degrees. Beat eggs, water, butter, peanut butter, and half the cake mix with electric mixer until light and fluffy. Stir in remaining cake mix and chocolate chips. Drop by rounded teaspoons on ungreased baking sheet. Bake for 10 to 12 minutes.

Day 194

Nicole's Blue Ribbon Cereal Squares
• •

1 cup light corn syrup
1 cup sugar
1½ cups peanut butter
1 teaspoon vanilla
8 cups crispy rice cereal
1 (12 ounce) package butterscotch chips
1 (6 ounce) package chocolate chips

*Bring corn syrup and sugar to a boil. Remove
from heat and add peanut butter, vanilla, and
cereal. Put mixture in 9x13-inch buttered pan
and press down. In double broiler melt chips.
Pour over cereal mixture and spread out.
Allow to set up at room temperature before
cutting into squares and serving.*

Day 195

Nutty Bars
· · · · · · · · · ·

½ cup butter
1½ cups graham cracker crumbs
1 (14 ounce) can sweetened condensed milk
1 (6 ounce) package semisweet chocolate chips
1⅓ cups flaked coconut
1 cup chopped peanuts

*Preheat oven to 350 degrees. Melt butter in
9x13-inch pan. Sprinkle crumbs evenly over
melted butter; pour sweetened condensed milk
evenly over crumbs. Top evenly with remaining
ingredients; press down firmly with fork.
Bake for 25 minutes or until lightly
browned. Cool and cut into bars.*

Day 196

Chocolate Cheesecake Bars

2 tubes refrigerated chocolate chip cookie dough
1 (12 ounce) package milk chocolate chips
2 (8 ounce) packages cream cheese
2 eggs
1 teaspoon vanilla

*Grease 9x13-inch pan. Press 1 tube of cookie
dough evenly into pan, forming crust. Melt
chocolate chips in microwave for 30 seconds.
Stir. Repeat until creamy. Blend cream cheese,
eggs, and vanilla until smooth. Fold in melted
chocolate. Layer over dough in pan.
Cut second tube of cookie dough in ¼-inch slices.
Place on top of chocolate cream cheese mixture.
Cover completely to form crust.
Bake at 350 for 30 minutes. Chill.*

Day 197

A Bite of Chocolate
• • • • • • • • • • • • • • • •

The appetite is sharpened by the first bites.

José Rizal

Day 198

Chocolate Cookie Bars

· · · · · · · · · · · · · · · · · ·

2 cups finely crushed
chocolate sandwich cookies
¼ cup butter, melted
1 (12 ounce) package semisweet chocolate chips
1 (14 ounce) can sweetened condensed milk
1 teaspoon vanilla

*Preheat oven to 350 degrees. Combine crushed
cookies and butter; press firmly on bottom of
9x13-inch baking pan. In medium saucepan over
medium heat, melt 1 cup chocolate chips with
condensed milk and vanilla. Pour evenly over
crust mix and sprinkle with remaining chips.
Bake for 20 minutes or until set. Cool. Cut into
bars. Store tightly covered at room temperature.*

Day 199

Chocolate Citrus Cooler
· · · · · · · · · · · · · · · · · · · ·

1½ cups chilled milk
¼ cup orange juice concentrate, thawed
3 tablespoons chocolate syrup
1 scoop vanilla or chocolate ice cream

*Place all ingredients in blender and blend
until smooth. Serve over crushed ice.*

Day 200

Double Fudge Nut Bars
. . . .

1¾ cups flour
¾ cup powdered sugar
¼ cup cocoa
1 cup cold butter
1 (12 ounce) package semisweet chocolate chips
1 (14 ounce) can sweetened condensed milk
1 teaspoon vanilla
1 cup chopped walnuts

*Preheat oven to 350 degrees. Mix flour,
powdered sugar, and cocoa. Cut in cold butter.
Press into 9x13-inch pan. Bake for 15 minutes.
Melt 1 cup chocolate chips in saucepan with
condensed milk and vanilla. When melted,
pour over crust. Sprinkle with remaining
chocolate chips and walnuts. Press down lightly.
Bake for 20 minutes.*

Day 201

Almond Roca Bars
. . . .

1 cup butter
½ cup sugar
½ cup brown sugar
1 egg, beaten
1 teaspoon vanilla
½ teaspoon almond extract
2 cups minus 2 tablespoons flour
1 (12 ounce) package chocolate chips
1 small package roasted almonds

*Preheat oven to 350 degrees. Cream butter
and sugars. Add remaining ingredients except
chocolate chips and almonds. Mix thoroughly and
spread on large cookie sheet. Bake for 10 to 12
minutes. Melt chocolate chips in microwave for
30 seconds. Stir. Repeat until creamy. Spread over
warm cookie and sprinkle almonds on top.
Cut into bars when cool.*

Day 202

Chocolate Mint Pudding
. . . .

½ cup sugar
3 tablespoons cornstarch
⅓ cup cocoa
¼ teaspoon salt
2½ cups milk
½ teaspoon vanilla
¼ teaspoon mint extract

In a saucepan, mix sugar, cornstarch, cocoa, and salt. Stir in milk and cook over medium heat, stirring constantly until thick. Stir and cook for 3 more minutes and stir in vanilla and mint extract. Chill. Top with whipped cream and a sprig of mint, if desired.

Day 203

Chocolate-Covered Coffee Beans

· ·

⅓ cup french roast coffee beans
½ cup milk chocolate chips

*Melt chocolate chips in microwave.
Mix in coffee beans. Place individual
beans on waxed paper to cool.*

Day 204

Fudge Frosting
. . . .

1 cup sugar
5 tablespoons butter or margarine
⅓ cup milk
1 cup chocolate chips

*Combine sugar, butter, and milk in saucepan.
Boil 1 minute, stirring constantly. Remove from
heat and stir in chips until smooth. Let thicken
slightly and pour over cookies, cakes, or ice cream.*

Day 205

Turtle Candies
. . . .

4 ounces pecan halves
24 caramels
1 teaspoon shortening
1 cup semisweet chocolate chips

*Preheat oven to 300 degrees. Cover cookie
sheet with aluminum foil, shiny side up. Lightly
grease foil with vegetable oil spray. Place 3
pecan halves in a Y shape on foil. Place 1 caramel
candy in center of each Y. Repeat. Bake just until
caramel is melted, about 9 to 10 minutes. Heat
shortening and chocolate chips over low heat just
until chocolate is melted. Spread over candies
and refrigerate for 30 minutes.*

Day 206

Rich Brownie Bars
. . . .

4 squares unsweetened baking chocolate
1 cup butter
2 cups sugar
1 cup flour
4 eggs, beaten
2 teaspoons hot coffee
1 cup semisweet chocolate chips
1 cup chopped nuts

Preheat oven to 325 degrees. Grease 9x13-inch baking pan. In small saucepan over low heat, melt chocolate and butter, stirring constantly. Remove from heat. In large bowl, combine sugar and flour. Add chocolate mixture, eggs, and coffee; stir until well blended. Stir in chocolate chips and nuts. Spread batter into prepared pan. Bake for 35 minutes. Refrigerate for 2 hours before serving. Cut into bars.

Day 207

Chocolate Cherry Bars
. . . .

1 fudge cake mix
1 teaspoon almond extract
1 large can cherry pie filling
2 eggs, beaten

*Combine all ingredients in a large bowl
until well mixed. Spray 9x13-inch pan with
cooking spray. Pour batter into pan and bake
at 350 degrees for 25 to 30 minutes. When cool,
add your favorite frosting or serve with
whipped topping or ice cream.*

Day 208

Reese's Squares
. . . .

2 sticks butter, melted
2½ cups peanut butter
5 cups powdered sugar
4 tablespoons butter, melted
1 cup semisweet chocolate chips

*Mix 2 sticks melted butter and peanut butter
until smooth. Add powdered sugar. Put into
a 9x13-inch baking pan. Pat down firmly.
Combine 4 tablespoons melted butter
and chocolate chips until smooth.
Spread on top of peanut butter mixture.
Refrigerate 2 hours. Cut into squares.*

Day 209

Mousse Pie
· · · · · · · · · ·

1 (8 ounce) package cream cheese, softened
½ cup cocoa
1 cup powdered sugar
1 teaspoon vanilla
2 cups whipped topping
1 prepared graham cracker crust

Beat cream cheese and cocoa in large bowl.
Add powdered sugar and blend well.
Stir in vanilla and whipped topping.
Pour into crust and chill until firm.

Day 210

Easy Chocolate Zucchini Cake
. . . .

1 box chocolate cake mix
½ teaspoon cinnamon
3 eggs
1¼ cups water
½ cup oil
1 cup shredded zucchini

Combine cake mix and cinnamon in large bowl.
Add eggs, water, and oil, and mix well.
Fold in zucchini. Pour batter into greased pan(s)
and spread evenly. Bake at 350 degrees for
50 to 60 minutes. Frost as desired.

Day 211

Speedy Brownies
. . . .

2 cups sugar
1¾ cups flour
½ cup cocoa
1 teaspoon salt
5 eggs
1 cup vegetable oil
1 teaspoon vanilla extract
1 cup semisweet chocolate chips

*In a mixing bowl, combine first 7 ingredients;
beat until smooth. Pour into a greased 9x13-inch
baking pan. Sprinkle with chocolate chips.
Bake at 350 degrees for 30 minutes, or until
a toothpick inserted near center comes out clean.
Cool in pan on a wire rack.*

Day 212

Chocolate Ice-Cream Delight
. . . .

1 cup milk
½ cup ice cubes
5 tablespoons chocolate syrup
¼ cup chocolate ice cream
2 tablespoons canned whipped topping

*Place milk, ice cubes, chocolate syrup,
and ice cream in blender; cover.
Blend until smooth. Pour into 2 glasses.
Top with whipped topping. Serve immediately.*

Day 213

Simplicity
. . . .

Make [food] simple and let
things taste of what they are.

CURNONSKY

Day 214

White Chocolate Mint Bark
· ·

1 pound white chocolate, chopped
15 to 20 peppermint candies, crushed

Melt chocolate in microwave or over low heat.
Mix melted chocolate and crushed mints.
Pour onto waxed paper. Cover with waxed paper.
Smooth the mixture to desired thickness
with a rolling pin. Allow to cool.
Break into pieces. Store in refrigerator.

Day 215

Cocoa Beef Tenderloin
. . . .

1 pound beef tenderloin
2 tablespoons butter, divided
½ teaspoon cocoa
1 clove garlic, finely chopped
¼ teaspoon dried rosemary leaves
¼ cup beef broth

*Cut beef into 1-inch slices. Heat 1 tablespoon
butter in skillet over medium-high heat. Sauté
beef for 4 to 5 minutes on each side, turning once,
until brown and center is medium rare. Remove
beef to warm platter; keep warm. Cook and stir
remaining butter, cocoa, garlic, and rosemary
in skillet until bubbly. Gradually stir in
beef broth. Heat to boiling; boil and stir
for 1 minute. Serve over beef.*

Day 216

Enjoyment
. . . .

It matters not how simple the food...
but let it be of good quality and properly cooked,
and everyone who partakes of it will enjoy it.

ALEXIS SOYER

Day 217

Snickerdoodle Cake
. . . .

1 German chocolate cake mix
1 (14 ounce) package caramels
1 stick margarine
⅓ cup milk
¾ cup chocolate chips
1 cup walnuts, chopped

Prepare cake mix, following package directions.
Pour half the batter into a greased 9x13-inch
greased pan. Bake at 350 degrees for 20 minutes.
Melt caramels with margarine and milk in
saucepan over low heat, stirring frequently.
Pour over baked cake. Sprinkle with chocolate
chips and nuts. Spoon remaining cake batter over
caramel layer. Bake at 250 degrees for 20 minutes.
Increase temperature to 350 degrees and bake
an additional 10 minutes.

Day 218

Chocolate Ice Cream Sauce
. . . .

1 (3 ounce) box chocolate pudding mix
1 (3 ounce) box butterscotch pudding mix
1 cup water
½ cup sugar
2 tablespoons butter

*Mix pudding mixes, water, and sugar
in a saucepan over low heat until thick.
Stir in butter. Serve over ice cream.*

Day 219

Dipped Cherries
. . . .

½ cup butter, melted
6 tablespoons corn syrup
1 (14 ounce) can sweetened condensed milk
1 teaspoon vanilla
3 pounds powdered sugar
3 (10 ounce) jars maraschino cherries, drained
2 cups semisweet chocolate chips
½ tablespoon butter

*In large mixing bowl, combine butter,
corn syrup, condensed milk, vanilla, and sugar.
Knead dough and form into walnut-sized balls
with cherry wrapped in middle. Place in freezer
to chill. In double boiler, melt chocolate chips
and butter. Dip chilled balls in chocolate.
Let cool on parchment paper.*

Day 220

Milk Chocolate Popcorn
. . . .

12 cups popcorn, popped
2½ cups salted peanuts
1 cup light corn syrup
1 (11½ ounce) package milk chocolate morsels
¼ cup butter or margarine

*Grease a large roasting pan. Line a large
bowl or serving plate with waxed paper.
Combine popcorn and nuts in prepared roasting
pan. Combine corn syrup, morsels, and butter
in medium, heavy-duty saucepan. Cook over
medium heat, stirring constantly, until mixture
boils. Pour over popcorn; toss well to coat. Bake
at 300 degrees, stirring frequently, for 30 to 40
minutes. Cool slightly in pan; remove to prepared
serving plate. Store in airtight container.*

Day 221

Melt in Your Mouth Toffee

. . . .

1 pound butter or margarine
1 cup sugar
1 cup brown sugar, packed
1 cup walnuts, chopped
2 cups semisweet chocolate chips

*In a heavy saucepan, combine butter and sugars.
Cook over medium heat, stirring constantly until
mixture boils. Boil to brittle stage, 300 degrees,
without stirring. Remove from heat. Pour nuts
and chocolate chips into a 9x13-inch dish. Pour
hot mixture over nuts and chocolate. Let mixture
cool and break into pieces before serving.*

Day 222

Rocky Road Squares
· · · · · · · · · · · · · · ·

3 pounds milk chocolate
½ pound butter, softened
10 ounces mini marshmallows
3 pounds peanuts

*Melt chocolate; stir until smooth. Add butter
and mix well (will be thick but warm).
Set in cold place until it thickens around edges.
Stir occasionally while cooling. Bring into warm
room and stir 5 to 10 minutes until creamy
and thinner. Add marshmallows and peanuts.
Pour on waxed paper-lined cookie sheet;
press ¾-inch thick. Cool. Cut in
squares at room temperature.*

Day 223

Cookie Truffles
. . . .

1 pound chocolate sandwich cookies, crushed
1 (8 ounce) package cream cheese, softened
2 cups semisweet chocolate chips, melted
¼ cup white chocolate chips, melted

*In large mixing bowl, combine crushed
cookies and cream cheese to form stiff dough.
Shape into balls. Using fork, dip balls into
melted chocolate. Place on wire rack over
waxed paper in a cool area until set.
Drizzle with melted white chocolate.*

Day 224

Easy Chocolate Pecan Pie
. . . .

2 eggs, room temperature
1 cup sugar
½ cup flour
½ cup butter, softened
1 teaspoon vanilla
1 cup semisweet chocolate chips
1 cup chopped pecans
1 unbaked 9-inch pie shell
Whipped topping

*Preheat oven to 350 degrees. Beat eggs at
high speed in a mixing bowl until thickened and
yellow. Beat in sugar gradually. Beat in flour
and butter at low speed. Stir in vanilla,
chocolate chips, and pecans. Spoon into pie shell.
Bake for 40 minutes or until golden brown.
Top with whipped topping.*

Day 225

Chocolate Truffles
. . . .
½ cup unsalted butter, softened
2½ cups powdered sugar, plus extra for topping
½ cup cocoa
¼ cup heavy cream
1½ teaspoons vanilla

CENTER:
Pecans, walnuts, almonds, or after-dinner mints

COATING:
Flaked coconut, crushed nuts, or powdered sugar

In large bowl, cream butter. In separate bowl, combine powdered sugar and cocoa; add to butter alternately with cream and vanilla. Blend well. Chill until firm. Shape small amount of mixture around desired center; roll into 1-inch ball. Drop into desired coating and turn until well covered. Chill until firm.

Day 226

Blackberry Bonbons
. . . .

1 cup white chocolate chips
1 (8 ounce) package cream cheese, softened
2 tablespoons blackberry preserves
1 (12 ounce) box vanilla wafers
8 ounces white chocolate candy coating, melted

*Melt chocolate chips and stir in cream cheese
and preserves. Crush cookies and add to chocolate
mixture. Shape into small balls, cool,
then coat with chocolate.*

Day 227

Chocolate Bar Dessert
. . . .

CRUST:

1 cup flour

2 tablespoons light brown sugar

½ cup butter, melted

½ cup chopped nuts

*Mix above ingredients together.
Press in 9x13-inch pan. Bake at 350 degrees
for 15 minutes. Cool.*

FILLING:

1 (8 ounce) package cream cheese

¾ cup powdered sugar

1 cup whipped topping

1 (5½ ounce) package instant chocolate pudding, prepared

Chocolate bars

*Combine cream cheese and powdered sugar.
Fold in whipped topping. Spread mixture
on crust. Top with chocolate pudding.
Spread 2 cups whipped topping over pudding.
Sprinkle with slivers of chocolate bars.
Refrigerate until set.*

Day 228

Be Inspired
. . . .

Take time in your day to be inspired by
something small—the scent of a flower from
your garden, a hug from a child, a bite of your
favorite chocolate dessert. . . . Then thank
God for the little things in life.

FROM *IN THE KITCHEN WITH MARY & MARTHA*

Day 229

Malted Milk Treats
. . . .

¼ cup instant malted milk powder
3 tablespoons milk
¼ cup light corn syrup
1 tablespoon butter
1 cup milk chocolate chips
½ cup semisweet chocolate chips
5 cups puffed cocoa cereal

*Heat milk powder and milk in a saucepan
over low heat. Stir in corn syrup and butter.
Heat to boiling, stirring constantly. Remove from
heat. Stir in chocolate chips until melted. Quickly
stir in cereal and blend well. Drop by tablespoons
onto waxed paper. Refrigerate for at least 1 hour.*

Day 230

Candy Bar Puffs
. . . .

4 teaspoons butter
1 cup boiling water
1 cup flour
Dash salt
4 eggs
Chocolate candy bars

*Melt butter in boiling water. Add flour and salt.
Stir vigorously. Cook and stir until mixture forms
a ball. Remove from heat and allow to cool
slightly. Add eggs and beat until smooth. Drop
dough by tablespoonfuls onto greased baking sheet.
Bake at 400 degrees for 15 to 20 minutes.
Remove puff from oven. Split open when
slightly cool and fill with candy bar pieces.*

White Chocolate Squares

1 (12 ounce) package
white chocolate chips,
divided
¼ cup butter or
margarine
2 cups flour
½ teaspoon baking
powder

1 teaspoon vanilla extract
1 (14 ounce) can
sweetened condensed
milk (not evaporated)
1 cup pecans or
walnuts, chopped
1 large egg
Powdered sugar

*In large saucepan over low heat, melt 1 cup
chips and butter. Stir in flour and baking powder
until blended. Stir in vanilla, sweetened
condensed milk, nuts, egg, and remaining chips.
Spoon mixture into greased 9x13-inch pan.
Bake 20 to 25 minutes at 350 degrees. Cool.
Sprinkle with powdered sugar; cut into squares.*

Day 232

Chocolate-Covered Strawberries
. . . .
½ cup semisweet chocolate chips
½ cup milk chocolate chips
1½ teaspoons shortening
1 pint fresh strawberries with stems

Melt chocolate with shortening over low heat.
Spear fruit with toothpicks; dip into the melted
chocolate. Place on waxed paper and cool.

Day 233

Fantastic White Fudge
. . . .

⅔ cup evaporated milk
1⅔ cups sugar
1½ cups white chocolate chips
1½ cups mini marshmallows
½ teaspoon salt
1 teaspoon vanilla extract

*Combine milk and sugar; bring to a boil
for 5 minutes. Add chocolate chips and
marshmallows. Stir until blended. Add salt
and vanilla and pour into a buttered
8-inch square baking dish to cool.*

Day 234

Malted Milkshakes
. . . .

1 cup milk
3 tablespoons malted milk powder
½ teaspoon vanilla
1 quart vanilla ice cream
½ cup milk chocolate chips

*Place milk and malted milk powder in blender
and process for 30 seconds. Add the vanilla,
ice cream, and chocolate chips and blend well.*

Day 235

Chicken in Cocoa Sauce
. . . .

2 pounds skinless, boneless chicken
¼ cup canola oil
1 large bell pepper, chopped
1 medium sweet onion, sliced
2 cloves garlic, minced
1 (16 ounce) can tomato sauce
½ teaspoon salt
1½ tablespoons chili powder
1 ounce baking chocolate
¼ teaspoon white pepper

*Brown chicken in oil and remove from pan.
Sauté pepper, onion, and garlic until done.
Add remaining ingredients. Stir until chocolate
is melted. Add chicken, and simmer on low heat
until chicken is tender. Serve with rice.*

Day 236

Nutty Fudge
. . . .

1 pound powdered sugar, sifted
1 stick real butter, sliced
½ cup cocoa
¼ cup milk
1½ teaspoon vanilla extract
½ cup nuts, chopped

*Dump powdered sugar, butter slices, cocoa,
and milk into microwave-safe bowl. Microwave
on high for 2 minutes. Remove; stir vigorously to
blend. Add vanilla and nuts. Pour into an
8-inch square pan lined with foil and
buttered. Refrigerate until firm.*

Day 237

Chocolate Brittle Surprise

. . . .

35 unsalted soda crackers
1 cup butter
1 cup brown sugar, packed
2 cups semisweet chocolate chips
1 cup pecans, chopped (optional)

*Cover cookie sheet with foil. Spray foil
with cooking oil spray. Place crackers on foil in
5x7-inch rows. Microwave butter on high for 2
minutes. Add brown sugar and stir. Microwave
on high for 2 more minutes, stirring every 30
seconds. Pour over crackers. Bake 17 minutes
at 350 degrees until bubbly. Sprinkle chocolate
chips over hot crackers. Spread after 2 minutes.
Sprinkle pecans on top. Refrigerate 1 hour.
Break into pieces. Can be frozen.*

Day 238

Choco-Butterscotch Crisps
. . . .

1 cup butterscotch chips
½ cup peanut butter
4 cups crispy rice cereal
1 cup chocolate chips
2 tablespoons butter
1 tablespoon water
½ cup powdered sugar

*Melt butterscotch chips and peanut butter
over very low heat, stirring occasionally.
Add cereal and mix well. Press half of mixture in
an 8x8-inch square pan and chill. Melt chocolate
chips, butter, and water in top of a double boiler
and add powdered sugar. Spread over chilled
mixture and press in remainder of
cereal mixture. Cut and chill.*

Day 239

Chocolate Pecan Tassies

. . . .

½ cup butter
1 (3 ounce) package cream cheese
1 cup flour

*Cream butter and cream cheese. Add flour;
refrigerate 1 hour. Form into 24 small balls
and press into small muffin tins.*

FILLING:

¾ cup brown sugar
1 egg, well beaten
1 tablespoon butter,
melted
2 cups chocolate chips

1 teaspoon vanilla
extract
Pinch salt
¾ to 1 cup pecans,
chopped

*Pour filling mixture into shells.
Bake at 350 degrees for 25 minutes.*

Day 240

Amaretto Fudge Cappuccino

. . . .

1 cup boiling water
1 tablespoon instant coffee granules
2 tablespoons amaretto-flavored creamer
1 tablespoon chocolate syrup

Combine water and coffee in mug;
stir until coffee is dissolved. Stir in creamer
and chocolate syrup. Serve immediately.

Day 241

Swedish No-Bake Chocolate Balls

. . . .

3 sticks margarine
2 cups sugar
3 tablespoons dark coffee (liquid)
3 tablespoons cocoa
3 teaspoons vanilla extract
5 cups quick oats
Coconut and colored sprinkles

*Mix all ingredients in a bowl and
form into ¾-inch balls. Dip in coconut
and colored sprinkles. Refrigerate.*

Day 242

Stress-Free!
· · · · · · · · · ·

When you're feeling overwhelmed,
try these great stress busters:

Take a walk.
Read your Bible.
Pray.
Read a book for a quick escape to
another world. Hug your spouse and your kids.
(Squeeze tightly!) Laugh. (Even better when
done with a friend.) And, of course,
take a big bite of something chocolate!

**FROM *IN THE KITCHEN*
*WITH MARY & MARTHA: ONE-DISH WONDERS***

Day 243

Chocolate-Covered Orange Balls
• •

1 pound powdered sugar
1 (12 ounce) package vanilla wafers, crushed
1 cup walnuts, chopped
¼ pound butter
1 (6 ounce) can frozen
orange juice concentrate, thawed
1½ pounds milk chocolate, melted

*In a large bowl, combine powdered sugar,
vanilla wafers, walnuts, butter, and orange juice.
Mix well and shape into 1-inch round balls;
allow to dry for 1 hour. Place chocolate chips in
top of double boiler. Stir frequently over medium
heat until melted. Dip balls into melted chocolate
and place in decorative paper cups.*

Day 244

Chocolate Graham Cracker Balls
. . . .

1 cup peanut butter
¾ cup powdered sugar
1 cup graham cracker crumbs
2 cups semisweet chocolate chips
3 (1 ounce) squares semisweet chocolate, chopped
1 tablespoon shortening

In a medium bowl, mix together peanut butter and powdered sugar until smooth. Stir in graham cracker crumbs until well blended. Form dough into 1-inch balls by rolling in your hands, or by using a cookie scoop. Melt semisweet chocolate chips, semisweet chocolate squares, and shortening in top half of a double boiler. Dip balls into melted chocolate and place on waxed paper to cool.

Day 245

White Chocolate Strawberry Trifle

· ·

2 pints fresh strawberries, washed and sliced
½ cup sugar
2 small boxes instant white
chocolate pudding mix
1½ cups milk
1 (8 ounce) container whipped topping
1 yellow cake mix, prepared and
cut into small squares
1 white chocolate bar, grated

Cover strawberries with sugar. Refrigerate.
Mix white chocolate pudding mix in a bowl
with the milk. Fold in the whipped topping.
In a large serving bowl, layer the cake squares,
strawberries, and then pudding mixture.
Refrigerate for at least 1 hour.
Top with grated white chocolate shavings.

Day 246

Chocolate-Dipped Cherries
· ·

¼ cup semisweet chocolate chips
¼ cup milk chocolate chips
1 teaspoon shortening
Maraschino cherries with stems

*Melt chocolate chips with shortening in
microwave on high for 1½ minutes. Stir until
smooth and dip cherries halfway up in chocolate.
Place on waxed paper and refrigerate until set.*

Day 247

Hot Cappuccino
· · · · · · · · · · · · · ·

1 cup instant hot chocolate mix
½ cup instant coffee granules (good quality)
½ cup powdered nondairy coffee creamer
½ cup powdered skim milk
1¼ teaspoons cinnamon
¼ teaspoon nutmeg
Boiling water
Chocolate, grated (optional)

*Mix dry ingredients well. Use ¼ cup mixture
for each 2 cups boiling water. Blend desired
amount until foamy and pour into mugs.
Sprinkle with grated chocolate if desired.*

Day 248

Rejoice and Be Glad
. . . .

The LORD has done it this very day;
let us rejoice today and be glad.

PSALM 118:24

Day 249

Chocolate Coffee Dessert
. . . .

Graham cracker squares (not crumbs)
2 cups (1 pint) whipping cream
½ cup powdered sugar
4 tablespoons chocolate syrup
1 tablespoon instant coffee granules
Chocolate garnish (chocolate shavings
or chocolate sprinkles)

*Place layer of graham crackers in 9x9-inch
baking pan. Whip cream; add powdered sugar,
chocolate syrup, and coffee. Place one-third of
mixture on crackers. Repeat with another layer
of crackers and second one-third of mixture;
top with third layer of crackers and last
one-third of mixture. Garnish with chocolate.*

Day 250

Chocolate Fondue
. . . .

1½ ounces unsweetened chocolate squares
¼ cup milk chocolate chips
1 tablespoon butter
1 cup sugar
1 (5 ounce) can evaporated milk
Toothpicks
Desired fruit

*Melt chocolate and butter over low heat
in a saucepan. Stir in sugar and slowly stir in
milk. Stir over heat continuously until sugar is
dissolved. Keep warm. Slice fruit such as bananas,
apples, strawberries, etc., and place them on
toothpicks. Dip into the fondue and enjoy.*

Day 251

Pamela's Chocolate
Cake in Minutes!
. . . .

1 chocolate cake mix (no pudding in mix)
1 (8 ounce) can soda pop (any flavor)
1 small tub whipped topping
1 candy bar (any flavor)

*Mix first two ingredients together in a
microwavable bowl (at least 8-cup size).
Microwave 8 to 12 minutes depending on
wattage. Spread chocolate frosting on top.
Garnish with whipped topping in your favorite
design. Crumble candy bar, sprinkle on top.*

Day 252

Truffle Mugs
. . . .

4 cups very hot, strong coffee
8 dark chocolate truffles, cut into quarters
Whipped topping for garnish

*Pour coffee into 4 festive mugs and place
truffle pieces in bowl. Spoon whipped topping into
serving dish. Serve coffee to your guests and
invite them to stir truffle pieces into their coffee.
Coffee should be stirred constantly until truffles
have melted. Guests can garnish their
drinks with whipped topping if desired.*

Day 253

Cocoa Pecans
· · · · · · · · · · ·

½ cup pecan halves
Warm water
Hot cocoa mix

Preheat oven to 350 degrees. Soak pecans in water for a few minutes. Drain pecans of excess water but do not dry. Toss pecans in cocoa mix until well coated. Spread on lightly greased cookie sheet. Bake for about 5 minutes or until lightly toasted and crusty.

Day 254

Chocolate Candy Caramel Bars
. . . .

1 box chocolate cake mix with pudding
½ cup shortening
1 cup evaporated milk, divided
1 package soft caramels
1 (14 ounce) bag candy-coated chocolate pieces

Grease 9x13-inch pan. Combine cake mix, shortening, and ⅔ cup evaporated milk. Mix well. Spread half the batter in pan. Bake for 15 minutes at 350 degrees. Combine caramels and ⅓ cup evaporated milk and heat in microwave until smooth. Sprinkle 1 cup candy-coated chocolate pieces over batter. Drizzle with caramel mixture. Spoon remaining batter over caramel. Add remaining candy-coated chocolate pieces. Bake for 25 minutes. Cool. Cut into bars.

Day 255

Chocolate Cola Cake
· · · · · · · · · · · · · · · · ·

1 box chocolate cake mix
1⅓ cups cola soda drink
¼ cup powdered sugar

*Prepare cake mix as directed replacing the
water with the cola. Bake according to
instructions. Allow to cool for several minutes.
Sprinkle with powdered sugar and serve.*

Day 256

White Chocolate–Dipped Strawberries
· · · · · · · · · ·

1 pint fresh strawberries, washed and dried
4 ounces white chocolate chips

*Melt chocolate chips in microwave or in
saucepan on low heat. Dip strawberries in
chocolate and place on waxed paper to cool.*

Day 257

Minty Chocolate Milk
. . . .

2 tablespoons chocolate syrup
⅛ teaspoon peppermint extract
1 cup milk
1 scoop chocolate ice cream

*Stir together chocolate syrup,
peppermint flavoring, and milk.
Add ice cream. Serve immediately.*

Day 258

White Chocolate Truffles
. . . .

1 (16 ounce) package white
chocolate candy melts or chips
⅔ cup heavy cream
2 teaspoons almond extract

*In a double boiler, heat chocolate
and cream, stirring until completely melted.
Remove from heat and add flavoring. Pour into
bowl and allow to cool in refrigerator until firm.
Use melon-baller or teaspoon to scoop small
amount of mixture. Roll into balls. Place on
cookie sheet covered with waxed paper.
Allow truffles to set before sharing.*

Day 259

A Daily Reminder
· · · · · · · · · · · · · · ·

Make a list of all the things for which
you're thankful. Write it on pretty stationery
and display it on the refrigerator where
you'll see it often—a daily reminder of
everything that's good in your life.

Day 260

Chocolate Waffles
. . . .

1 cup waffle mix
Dash salt
¼ cup unsweetened cocoa
⅔ cup milk
1 egg

*Combine waffle mix, salt, and cocoa.
Add milk and egg and blend well. Bake in hot
waffle iron until done. Top with whipped cream
and strawberry ice-cream topping.*

Favorite Chocolate Chip Cookies

⅔ cup shortening
⅔ cup butter (no substitutions)
1 cup sugar
1 cup packed brown sugar
2 eggs
2 teaspoons vanilla
3 cups flour
1 teaspoon baking soda
1 teaspoon salt
1 (12 ounce) package semisweet chocolate chips

*Preheat oven to 375 degrees. Cream shortening,
butter, sugars, eggs, and vanilla. Add flour,
baking soda, and salt. Mix in chocolate chips.
Drop 1-inch spoonfuls on ungreased
cookie sheet and bake for approximately
8 minutes or until golden brown.*

Day 262

Chocolate Strawberry Pie
. . . .

½ cup milk chocolate chips
½ cup semisweet chocolate chips
3 tablespoons milk
1 teaspoon vanilla
1 deep-dish piecrust, baked
1 (6 ounce) package frozen
strawberries in syrup, thawed
1 (8 ounce) container whipped topping

*Combine chocolate chips and milk in
microwavable bowl. Microwave on medium
for 1½ minutes, stirring every 30 seconds until
completely melted. Stir in vanilla. Pour chocolate
into baked piecrust. Mix strawberries and
whipped topping. Spread over chocolate.
Allow to cool in refrigerator.*

Day 263

Chocolate Cookies
· · · · · · · · · · · · ·

⅔ cup powdered sugar
½ cup butter or margarine, softened
½ teaspoon vanilla
1 cup flour
2 tablespoons cocoa
⅛ teaspoon salt

Beat together powdered sugar, butter, and vanilla at medium speed. Reduce speed and add flour, cocoa, and salt. Divide dough in half. One half at a time, place dough between sheets of lightly floured waxed paper and roll out to ⅛-inch thickness, refrigerating remaining half. Remove paper and cut dough with 2- to 2½-inch cookie cutters. Place on ungreased cookie sheets. Bake at 325 degrees for 14 to 18 minutes. Cool cookies completely before decorating with icing as desired.

Day 264

Strawberries with Chocolate Crème

1 cup milk chocolate chips
1 cup semisweet chocolate chips
1 (8 ounce) package cream cheese, softened
2 pints strawberries, washed, stemmed, and dried

*Melt chocolate in the microwave for
1½ minutes, stirring frequently until smooth.
Blend the melted chocolate with the cream cheese.
Place in a decorator's icing bag and pipe into
strawberries. Keep refrigerated.*

Day 265

Chocolate Rum Truffles
. . . .

6 (1 ounce) squares dark semisweet chocolate
3 tablespoons unsalted butter
2 tablespoons powdered sugar
3 egg yolks
1 tablespoon rum flavoring
½ cup semisweet chocolate, finely grated

Melt chocolate squares in top of double boiler over boiling water. Blend in butter and sugar, stirring until sugar dissolves. Remove from heat and add egg yolks one at a time, beating well after each addition. Stir in rum flavoring. Place in bowl covered with waxed paper overnight, but do not chill. Shape into 1-inch balls and roll in grated chocolate. Best served after a day or two.

Day 266

Chocolate Malt Shake

. . . .

1 cup milk
2 tablespoons malted milk powder
1½ cups chocolate ice cream

Blend together well and serve.

Day 267

Choco Punch
. . . .

4 (1 ounce) squares semisweet chocolate
½ cup sugar
2 cups hot water
2 quarts milk
1½ teaspoons vanilla
1 quart vanilla ice cream
1 quart club soda
½ pint heavy whipping cream, whipped
Cinnamon

*In saucepan, combine chocolate and sugar
with hot water. Bring to a boil, stirring for
approximately 3 minutes. Add milk; continue
heating. When hot, beat in vanilla. Remove
from heat. Chill; then pour into a punch bowl
over ice cream. For sparkle, add club soda.
Top with whipped cream and cinnamon.*

Day 268

White Chocolate Fruit Trifle
. . . .

1 box yellow cake mix, prepared
2 (4 ounce) boxes instant white
chocolate pudding, prepared
1 can cherry pie filling
2 (8 ounce) containers frozen
whipped topping, thawed
½ cup blueberries, washed and dried

*Cut cake into small squares. Layer cake,
pudding, cherry pie filling, and whipped topping.
Repeat. Top with blueberries.*

Day 269

Easy Cake Mix Cookies

· · · · · · · · · · · · · · · · · · · ·

1 box cake mix (any flavor)
1 large egg
¼ cup oil
¼ cup water
1 cup any or all of the following: chopped nuts,
raisins, oatmeal, coconut, chocolate chips, or
candy-coated chocolate pieces

*Preheat oven to 350 degrees. Combine cake mix,
egg, oil, and water. Beat until well blended.
Stir in remaining ingredient(s). Drop by
teaspoons about 1 inch apart on greased cookie
sheet. Bake for 12 to 15 minutes or until done.*

Day 270

Cookies and Cream Pie
. . . .

8 to 10 chocolate
sandwich cookies

1 (9-inch) prepared
chocolate cookie crust

4 ounces cream cheese,
softened

2 tablespoons white sugar

1 tablespoon milk

1 (8 ounce) container
frozen whipped topping,
thawed

2 (3.9 ounce) packages
instant vanilla
pudding mix

2 cups milk

Place 8 to 10 cookies on the bottom of the piecrust.
Combine cream cheese, sugar, and 1 tablespoon milk
in a large bowl. Beat until smooth. Gently fold in
half of the whipped topping. Spread on the bottom of
crust. Then combine pudding mix with 2 cups milk.
Beat with wire whisk for 2 minutes. Spread over
cream cheese layer. Refrigerate 4 hours or until set.
Top with remaining whipped topping
and a few crumbled cookies.

Day 271

Chocolate Malt Cake
. . . .
1 (18 ounce) box chocolate cake mix
¾ cup instant malted milk powder, divided
1 (16 ounce) can prepared vanilla frosting

Prepare cake according to package
directions adding ½ cup malted milk powder.
Bake as directed. Stir in remaining
¼ cup of malted milk powder into
vanilla frosting and frost cake
after it has cooled.

Day 272

Decadence...
. . . .

Enjoy a decadent chocolate dessert somewhere
other than the kitchen. . . . Get out there and
savor your dessert with a view of the sunset,
in front of a blazing fire, on the front porch
during a rain shower, or in the woods
on a soft picnic blanket.

Day 273

Moist Double-Chocolate Cake
. . . .

1 (18 ounce) box chocolate cake mix
1 cup sour cream
½ cup water
½ cup chocolate milk
⅓ cup vegetable oil
3 eggs

Combine all ingredients and mix well.
Bake as directed on box. Cool and frost as desired.

Day 274

Chocolate–Covered Pretzels
. . . .
1 cup milk chocolate chips
1 bag pretzel twists

Melt chocolate chips in microwave on high for 1½ minutes, stirring often until smooth. Dip pretzels in chocolate until completely coated. Remove using pair of tongs. Place on waxed paper to cool.

Day 275

Beef Curry
· · · · · · · · ·

1 pound stew beef, cut into cubes
3 tablespoons olive oil
2 tablespoons curry powder
1 ounce unsweetened chocolate
¼ cup molasses
¼ cup tomato sauce
4 cups orange juice
1 cup water
Salt and pepper to taste

Brown stew meat in oil until light brown.
Add curry and continue browning. Add
remaining ingredients and bring to a boil.
Simmer for 1 hour, adding the water
as needed. Serve with rice.

Day 276

Chocolate Puffs
• • • • • • • • • • • • •

4 teaspoons butter (no substitutions)
1 cup boiling water
1 cup flour
Dash salt
4 eggs
Milk chocolate bar pieces

Melt butter in boiling water. Add flour and salt.
Stir vigorously. Cook and stir until mixture forms
a ball that doesn't separate. Remove from heat
and allow to cool slightly. Add eggs and beat until
smooth. Drop dough onto greased baking sheet,
using 1 tablespoon dough. Bake at 400 degrees
for 20 minutes. Remove from oven and split.
Fill with milk chocolate bar pieces.

Day 277

Simplicity
· · · · · · · ·

In cooking, as in all the arts,
simplicity is the sign of perfection.

CURNONSKY

Chili Con Carne
• • • • • • • • • • • • •

1 pound ground beef
1 cup chopped onion
¾ cup chopped green pepper
1 (16 ounce) can diced tomatoes
1 (16 ounce) can pinto beans, drained
1 (8 ounce) can tomato sauce
1 (2 ounce) square unsweetened chocolate
1 teaspoon salt
1 teaspoon chili powder
1 bay leaf

*Cook meat, onion, and green pepper in a
heavy skillet. Cook until meat is lightly browned
and vegetables are tender. Stir in remaining
ingredients. Cover and simmer for
1 hour. Remove bay leaf.*

Day 279

Decadent Chocolate Cake
. . . .

2 cups sugar
½ cup butter (no substitutions)
2 eggs, beaten
4 ounces unsweetened chocolate
1½ cups milk
2 cups sifted cake flour
2 teaspoons baking powder, rounded
1 teaspoon salt
2 teaspoons vanilla

Cream sugar and butter. Add eggs. Add melted chocolate. Sift dry ingredients and alternately add with liquid. Add vanilla and mix. Bake in loaf pans at 350 degrees for 40 to 50 minutes or for 1 hour in 8-inch round pans. Top with your favorite icing.

Day 280

Chocolate Mocha Icing
. . . .

3 ounces cream cheese
2 cups powdered sugar
Pinch salt
2 ounces unsweetened chocolate, melted
1½ teaspoons vanilla
3 tablespoons brewed coffee

Cream cheese, sugar, and salt until fluffy.
Stir in melted chocolate; add vanilla and coffee.

Day 281

Movie Mix
· · · · · · · · ·

2 cups peanuts, roasted and salted
1 cup candy-covered chocolate pieces
1 cup raisins

Mix together; place in bowl and serve.

Day 282

Colorado Chicken Mole

. . . .

½ cup flour
¼ cup oil
1 tablespoon chili powder
2 (14 ounce) cans chicken broth
1 to 2 ounce envelope chili mix
¼ teaspoon garlic salt
1 to 2 ounce block Mexican chocolate
6 boneless and skinless chicken breasts

*Fry the flour in the ¼ cup oil. Add the chili
powder and cook slowly for 1 minute. Add the
chicken broth, chili mix, garlic salt, and chocolate.
Add chicken breasts and simmer for 45 minutes
over medium to low heat until tender
and no longer pink in center.*

Day 283

Chocolate Spritz Cookies
. . . .

1¼ cups butter, softened
1 cup sugar
⅔ cup dark brown sugar
2 large eggs
1 teaspoon vanilla
½ teaspoon baking soda
¼ teaspoon salt
⅔ cup cocoa
2½ cups flour

Cream butter and sugars until light and fluffy. Add eggs one at a time. Add vanilla. In separate bowl, combine baking soda, salt, cocoa, and flour; add gradually to creamed mixture until just blended. Use cookie press fitted with disk of choice. Press cookies 2 inches apart onto ungreased cookie sheets. Bake at 375 degrees for 10 minutes.

Day 284

Health Mix
· · · · · · · · · ·

2 cups almonds, roasted and salted
2 cups granola
1 cup yogurt-covered raisins
1 cup dark chocolate chips

Mix together; place in bowl and serve.

Day 285

Cereal Bread
. . . .

1 cup frosted corn
flakes
2 cups milk
2 cups sugar
2 eggs
1 teaspoon vanilla

3½ cups flour
1 teaspoon baking soda
2 teaspoons baking
powder
½ cup semisweet
chocolate chips

Preheat oven to 350 degrees. Soak cereal in milk for 10 minutes. In large bowl, beat sugar and eggs. Add cereal mixture and vanilla. Sift flour with baking soda and baking powder and stir thoroughly into cereal mixture. Add chocolate chips and mix well. Pour into 2 greased 5x9-inch loaf pans and bake for about 45 minutes or until toothpick inserted in center comes out clean.

Day 286

Shara's Peppermint Bark
· ·

1 (12 ounce) bag of chocolate chips
1 (12 ounce) package white
chocolate cooking/baking bark
2 to 3 candy canes, crushed
½ cup pecans, chopped

*Melt chocolate chips and pour into a greased
8x8-inch dish. Melt white chocolate bark and
pour over the top of the chocolate mixture.
Sprinkle both the candy cane and nut pieces onto
the warm chocolate mixture. Refrigerate for
a few hours. Break into pieces. Store in the
fridge or freeze for up to 6 months.*

Day 287

Fall Flavors Chili
· · · · · · · · · · · · · ·

2 pounds ground beef, browned and drained

1 quart water

1 large sweet onion, diced

2 (8 ounce) cans tomato sauce

3 cloves garlic

1 teaspoon allspice

½ teaspoon red pepper

1 teaspoon ground cumin seed

1½ teaspoons salt

4 tablespoons chili powder

½ ounce unsweetened chocolate

1 bay leaf

2 tablespoons vinegar

1 teaspoon ground cloves

2 teaspoons Worcestershire sauce

1 teaspoon cinnamon

Combine all ingredients. Stir to blend; bring to a boil; reduce heat and simmer uncovered for about 3 hours. Remove bay leaf. Serve alone or with spaghetti. Top with shredded cheese.

Day 288

Peter's Treats
. . . .

1 cup butter, softened (no substitutions)
1 cup powdered sugar
1 teaspoon vanilla
1¼ cups flour
1 cup quick oats
Dash salt
Chocolate star candies

*Cream butter, powdered sugar, and vanilla.
Stir in flour, oats, and salt. Shape dough into
2 rolls. Wrap and seal in waxed paper. Chill for
at least 2 hours. Preheat oven to 350 degrees.
Cut dough into ¼-inch slices and place on
ungreased cookie sheets. Top each with
chocolate star. Bake for 10 to 12 minutes.*

Day 289

Easy Chocolate Pizza Bars
. . . .

1 tube refrigerated chocolate chip cookie dough
½ cup peanut butter
1 cup milk chocolate chips
Assorted candy bars

*Press cookie dough into round pizza pan
or 9x13-inch pan and bake as directed.
Immediately after removing from oven, drop
peanut butter onto pizza. Sprinkle chocolate chips
on top. Wait about 2 minutes until peanut butter
and chocolate chips begin to melt; then spread.
Chop up assorted candy bars and
sprinkle on top. Cut into bars.*

Day 290

Together Time
. . . .

Gather your family together once a week for
devotions and dessert. Read through a family-
friendly devotional book or study a passage from
the Bible. End with prayer and a sweet treat!

**FROM *IN THE KITCHEN WITH
MARY & MARTHA: ONE-DISH WONDERS***

Day 291

Cookies and Cream Pie

1 (3.9 ounce) box chocolate instant pudding mix
1 (8 ounce) container frozen
whipped topping, thawed
1½ cups chocolate sandwich cookie crumbs
1 (9 inch) prepared chocolate crumb piecrust

*Prepare pudding according to pie filling directions
on package; allow to set. When pudding is ready,
fold in whipped topping. Add cookie crumbs; stir.
Pour mixture into prepared piecrust. Freeze pie
until firm. Thaw in refrigerator before serving.*

Day 292

Cocoa Chicken
. . . .

1 green bell pepper, chopped
1 large onion, chopped
2 cloves garlic
¼ cup vegetable oil
1 (16 ounce) can tomato sauce
½ teaspoon salt
1 tablespoon chili powder
¼ teaspoon pepper
1 (1 ounce) square baking chocolate
2 pounds of boneless, skinless chicken breast

Cook pepper, onion, and garlic in oil until onion becomes translucent. Add tomato sauce and salt. Add seasonings and chocolate. Stir until chocolate is melted, add chicken, and simmer on low heat until chicken is very tender and no longer pink in the center. Serve over rice or noodles.

Day 293

Caramel Walnut Bites

. . . .

3 cups milk chocolate candy coating
1 cup walnuts
1 cup caramel baking balls

Melt chocolate and stir in other ingredients.
Drop by spoonful onto waxed paper
and let set up in refrigerator.

Day 294

Minty Hot Chocolate
· · · · · · · · · · · · · · · · · · · ·

4 cups boiling water
1⅓ cups hot chocolate mix
¼ to ½ teaspoon peppermint
extract, according to taste
4 candy canes
Marshmallows

*Mix water, hot chocolate mix, and extract.
Pour into 4 mugs. Serve each with a candy
cane for stirring and marshmallows.*

Day 295

Country Chocolate Cookies

. . . .

1½ cups sugar
½ cup shortening
3 eggs
2 cups flour
½ teaspoon baking soda
½ teaspoon salt
½ cup cocoa powder
Powdered sugar

*In a large mixing bowl, cream sugar and
shortening. Add eggs, then sift in dry ingredients.
Chill. Shape into balls. Roll in powdered sugar.
Bake at 350 degrees for 8 to 10 minutes.*

Day 296

Twist of Orange Hot Chocolate
· ·

2 cups milk
3 (1x2 inch) orange peel
strips (orange part only)
⅛ teaspoon cinnamon
½ teaspoon instant espresso powder
4 ounces semisweet chocolate, grated

*Combine all ingredients in saucepan.
Stir over low heat until chocolate melts.
Increase heat and bring to a boil, stirring often.
Immediately remove from heat and whisk until
frothy. Return to heat and bring just to a boil
again. Repeat heating and whisking
once again. Discard orange peel.
Pour hot chocolate into two mugs.*

Day 297

Chocolate Fruit Mix
. . . .

1 cup mini chocolate chips
1 cup yogurt-covered raisins
1 cup dried fruit

Mix together; place in bowl and serve.

Day 298

Oatmeal Bars
. . . .

½ cup butter
⅓ cup fine sugar
1 tablespoon light corn syrup
4 cups oats
½ cup milk chocolate chips
½ cup semisweet chocolate chips

*Cook butter, sugar, and corn syrup
in saucepan and stir over low heat until
everything is melted and combined. Remove from
heat and stir in oatmeal. Add chocolate chips
and mix to combine. Place in a shallow,
greased 8x8-inch pan and press down well.
Bake at 350 degrees for 30 minutes.*

Day 299

Chocolate Mallow Drops
· ·

2 cups milk chocolate chips
2 ounces mini multicolored marshmallows
½ cup peanuts

Melt chocolate in microwave for
1½ minutes on high, stirring until smooth.
Add marshmallows and peanuts.
Place spoonfuls on waxed paper and cool.

Day 300

Crunchy Clusters

· · · · · · · · · · · · · ·

1 cup white chocolate chips
10 graham crackers, broken into small pieces
½ cup peanuts, chopped
½ cup semisweet chocolate chips

*Melt white chocolate in microwave for
1½ minutes on high, stirring until smooth.
Stir the crackers and peanuts into the white
chocolate. Drop by spoonfuls on waxed paper.
Melt the remaining chocolate chips and drizzle
with a fork over the clusters. Cool completely.*

Day 301

Chocolate Banana Cake Mix Cookies
. . . .

1 box banana cake mix
2 eggs
½ cup vegetable oil
1 cup milk chocolate chips

Preheat oven to 350 degrees.
Combine all ingredients in bowl and mix
well with spoon. Drop by heaping
tablespoons onto ungreased cookie sheet.
Bake for 8 to 10 minutes. Do not overbake.
Remove to wire rack to cool.

Day 302

Rejoice Always
. . . .

Rejoice in the Lord always.
I will say it again: Rejoice!

PHILIPPIANS 4:4

Day 303

Earthquake Cake
. . . .

1 cup nuts, chopped
1 cup flaked coconut, finely chopped
1 German chocolate cake mix
1 (8 ounce) package cream cheese, softened
1 cup shortening
1 pound powdered sugar

*Grease 9x13-inch baking pan; put nuts
and coconut in pan. Prepare cake mix according
to package directions and spread on top of nuts
and coconut. Then beat together cream cheese,
shortening, and powdered sugar until fluffy.
Drop by spoonfuls on top of cake batter in pan.
Bake at 350 degrees for 40 minutes
or until done when tested.*

Day 304

Chocolate Caramel Apples
. . . .

6 medium-sized apples,
washed and dried
6 Popsicle sticks
1 (14 ounce) package individually
wrapped caramels, unwrapped
2 tablespoons milk
1 (12 ounce) package mini chocolate chips

Wash apples and push one stick inside each apple.
In a microwavable bowl, place caramels and milk
in microwave and heat for 2 minutes, stirring
halfway. Allow to cool briefly. Roll each apple
quickly in caramel sauce until well coated.
Place on waxed paper. Sprinkle with
chocolate chips and allow to cool.

Day 305

Chocolate Chip Pumpkin Cookies
. . . .

1 teaspoon baking soda
1 teaspoon milk
1 cup pumpkin
¾ cup sugar
½ cup vegetable oil
1 egg
2 cups flour

2 teaspoons baking powder
1 teaspoon cinnamon
½ teaspoon salt
1 cup semisweet chocolate chips
1 teaspoon vanilla

Preheat oven to 375 degrees. Dissolve baking soda in milk and set aside. Combine pumpkin, sugar, oil, and egg; stir. Add flour, baking powder, cinnamon, salt, and baking soda mixture. Mix well. Stir in chocolate chips and vanilla. Spoon onto cookie sheet. Bake for 10 to 12 minutes. Do not to overbake.

Day 306

Chocolate Eggplant
. . . .

1 eggplant
2 tablespoons olive oil
1 cup semisweet chocolate chips

Cut eggplant into ¼-inch round slices.
Heat olive oil in skillet over medium heat.
Fry eggplant slices until golden brown.
Place on paper towel–lined plate.
Melt chocolate chips in small saucepan;
stir until smooth. Place eggplant on platter;
drizzle with melted chocolate and serve.

Day 307

Banana Chocolate Chip Cookies
. . . .

⅔ cup shortening

1 cup sugar

2 eggs

1 teaspoon vanilla

2¼ cups flour

2 teaspoons baking powder

¼ teaspoon baking soda

½ teaspoon salt

3 small ripe bananas, mashed

1 (12 ounce) package milk chocolate chips

Preheat oven to 400 degrees. Blend shortening and sugar. Add eggs one at a time, beating after each addition. Add vanilla. Combine dry ingredients and add to creamed mixture. Add mashed bananas and mix well. Stir in chocolate chips. Drop by teaspoons onto ungreased cookie sheet. Bake for 12 to 15 minutes. Makes 6 dozen.

Day 308

Melting Tip
· · · · · · · · ·

Chocolate has a very low melting point.
It doesn't do well at excessively high temperatures.
Always melt chocolate in a double boiler over
very low heat, never letting the water boil.

**FROM *IN THE KITCHEN WITH
MARY & MARTHA: COOKIN' UP CHRISTMAS***

Day 309

White Chocolate Mocha
· · · · · · · · · · · · · · · · · · · ·

1 cup milk
4 tablespoons white chocolate chips
1 cup of brewed espresso
Whipped topping

Heat milk in a saucepan over low heat.
Stir in chocolate chips until melted. Add coffee.
Pour into mugs and top with whipped cream.

Day 310

Nutty Chocolate Crescents

⅔ cup light brown sugar
⅔ cup butter
1 cup chopped pecans
1 (12 ounce) package chocolate chips
1 (8 ounce) tube refrigerated crescent rolls

*Bring sugar and butter to boil. Allow to cool.
Add nuts and chocolate chips. Place tablespoonfuls
inside individual unbaked crescent rolls and roll
up. Pinch to seal. Place on a lightly greased baking
pan. Bake at 375 degrees for 8 to 10 minutes
until golden brown. Do not overbake.*

Day 311

Creamy Dreamy Hot Chocolate
. . . .

1 (14 ounce) can sweetened condensed milk
½ cup unsweetened cocoa powder
2 teaspoons vanilla
⅛ teaspoon salt
6½ cups hot water

Combine first four ingredients in large saucepan;
mix well. Over medium heat, slowly stir in water.
Cook until heated through, stirring frequently.

Day 312

White Chocolate Pecans
. . . .

3 cups white chocolate chips
1 cup pecans
Cinnamon

Melt chocolate and stir in pecans.
Drop by spoonful onto waxed paper and sprinkle
lightly with cinnamon. Allow to cool.

Day 313

Dirt Cake
. . . .

1 (16 ounce) package chocolate sandwich cookies
1 (8 ounce) package cream cheese, softened
½ cup (1 stick) butter, softened
1 cup powdered sugar
1 (8 ounce) container whipped topping
2 (3 ounce) boxes vanilla instant pudding mix
3 cups milk
1 teaspoon vanilla

*Crush cookies and put half of crumbs in
9x13-inch baking pan. Mix cream cheese and
butter until smooth. Mix in powdered sugar.
Fold in whipped topping. In separate bowl,
mix pudding mixes, milk, and vanilla.
Fold in cream cheese mixture. Stir well.
Pour batter on top of crumbs. Sprinkle
remaining crumbs on top. Refrigerate.*

Day 314

Jake's Hot Cocoa
. . . .

1 cup water
2 squares unsweetened chocolate
½ cup sugar
3 cups milk
1 teaspoon vanilla

In medium saucepan over low heat, cook water and chocolate until chocolate is completely melted and mixture is well blended, stirring constantly with whisk. Add sugar; mix well. Bring to a boil over medium-high heat. Boil for 3 minutes, stirring constantly. Gradually add milk, stirring with whisk until well blended. Stir in vanilla. Reduce heat to medium. Cook until mixture is heated through, stirring occasionally.

Day 315

Banana S'more Snacks
. . . .

Graham cracker squares
Sliced bananas
Milk chocolate candy bars
Large marshmallows

*For each snack, top a graham cracker
with a piece of chocolate, a banana, and a
marshmallow. Microwave 10 to 12 seconds
or until puffed. Place another graham
cracker on top and enjoy.*

Day 316

White Chocolate Hot Cocoa
· · · · · · · · · · · · · · · · · · ·

3 cups half-and-half, divided
¾ cup white chocolate chips
3 cinnamon sticks
⅛ teaspoon nutmeg
1 teaspoon vanilla
¼ teaspoon almond extract
Cinnamon

In medium saucepan, combine ¼ cup half-and-half, white chocolate chips, cinnamon sticks, and nutmeg. Whisk over low heat until chocolate is melted. Remove cinnamon sticks. Add remaining half-and-half. Whisk until heated through. Remove from heat. Stir in vanilla and almond extract. Serve warm in cups or mugs. Sprinkle with cinnamon.

Day 317

Steaming Mocha Cocoa

. . . .

2 cups milk
2 tablespoons cocoa
2 tablespoons brown sugar
1 tablespoon ground coffee
1 teaspoon vanilla

Heat all ingredients in small saucepan
and whisk until steaming.
Strain and pour into 2 mugs.

Day 318

Superior Chocolate
· · · · · · · · · · · · · · · ·

The superiority of [hot] chocolate,
both for health and nourishment, will soon give
it the same preference over tea and coffee in
America which it has in Spain.

THOMAS JEFFERSON

Day 319

Cherry Nut Mix
· · · · · · · · · · ·

1 cup white chocolate chips
1 cup dried cherries
1 cup roasted almonds

Mix together; place in bowl and serve.

German Chocolate Bread
. . . .

2 boxes German chocolate cake mix
2 small boxes instant chocolate pudding mix
1 (12 ounce) container sour cream
10 eggs
1½ cups oil
½ cup water
1 (12 ounce) package
semisweet chocolate chips
1 cup flaked coconut

*Preheat oven to 325 degrees. Mix
together all ingredients. Pour into 3 greased
loaf pans. Bake for 1 hour or until toothpick
inserted in center comes out clean.*

Day 321

Toffee
· · · · · ·

1 cup chopped pecans
¾ cup packed brown sugar
½ cup margarine or butter
½ cup semisweet chocolate chips

*Butter 9x9x2-inch baking pan. Spread pecans
in bottom of pan. Bring brown sugar and
margarine to a boil, stirring constantly. Boil over
medium heat, and continue to stir for 7 minutes.
Remove from heat and immediately spread
mixture over pecans in pan. Sprinkle chocolate
chips over hot mixture and place cookie sheet
over pan until chocolate chips are melted.
Smooth melted chocolate over candy and cut
into ½-inch squares while hot.
Chill until firm. Yields 3 dozen candies.*

Day 322

No-Bake Peanut Butter Bars

· ·

2 cups graham cracker crumbs
1½ cups powdered sugar
1 cup chunky peanut butter
½ cup butter or margarine, melted
½ cup chopped salted peanuts
1½ cups milk chocolate chips

*Lightly grease an 11x7-inch baking pan and
set aside. Mix all ingredients except chocolate
chips in a large mixing bowl. Press mixture
into prepared pan. In a small saucepan, melt
chips over low heat, stirring constantly. Spread
chocolate evenly over bars. Chill until set, and cut.*

Day 323

Caramel Hot Cocoa
. . . .

2 cups milk
3 tablespoons caramel sauce
3 tablespoons chocolate sauce
Dash salt

Heat milk and add sauces.
Sprinkle with salt and mix well. Serve in mugs.

Day 324

Peanut Butter Bonbons
. . . .

1½ cups powdered sugar
1 cup graham cracker crumbs (about 12 squares)
½ cup margarine or butter
½ cup peanut butter chips
1 (6 ounce) package semisweet chocolate chips
1 tablespoon shortening

Combine powdered sugar and cracker crumbs.
Melt margarine and peanut butter chips over low
heat and stir into crumb mixture. Shape into
1-inch balls. Melt chocolate chips with
shortening and dip balls into chocolate with
tongs until coated. Place on waxed paper and
chill until firm. Yields 3 dozen candies.

Day 325

Crispy Cereal Chocolate Drops
. . . .

2 cups (12 ounces) butterscotch chips
1 cup (6 ounces) semisweet chocolate chips
½ cup salted peanuts
4 cups crisp cereal (almost anything will work)

*Melt butterscotch chips and chocolate chips
over very low heat stirring constantly until
smooth. Remove from heat. Add peanuts
and cereal. Stir carefully until well coated.
Drop by teaspoonfuls onto waxed paper.
Chill until firm. Yields 8 dozen.*

Day 326

World's Best Cocoa
. . . .

¼ cup cocoa
½ cup sugar
⅓ cup hot water
⅛ teaspoon salt
4 cups milk
¾ teaspoon vanilla

Mix cocoa, sugar, water, and salt in saucepan. Over medium heat, stir constantly until mixture boils. Continue to stir and boil for 1 minute. Add milk and heat. (Do not boil.) Remove from heat and add vanilla; stir well. Pour into four mugs and serve immediately.

Day 327

Chocolate Caramel Cookies

. . . .

1 box chocolate cake mix
2 eggs
½ cup vegetable oil
1 cup milk chocolate chips
12 caramels, chopped

Preheat oven to 350 degrees. Combine cake mix, eggs, and oil in bowl and mix well with spoon. Add chocolate chips and caramels. Drop by heaping tablespoons onto ungreased cookie sheet. Bake for 8 to 10 minutes. Do not overbake. Remove to wire rack to cool.

Day 328

Chocolate Pecan Pie

. . . .

2 (1 ounce) squares unsweetened chocolate
2 tablespoons butter
3 eggs
½ cup sugar
¾ cup dark corn syrup
1 cup pecans, halved
1 (9 inch) piecrust, unbaked

*Melt chocolate and butter together. Beat together
eggs, sugar, chocolate mixture, and corn syrup.
Mix in pecans. Pour into piecrust. Bake at 375
degrees for 40 to 50 minutes, just until set.
Serve slightly warm or cold with ice
cream or whipped topping.*

Day 329

Grand Mix
. . . .

1 cup milk chocolate chips
1 cup white chocolate chips
1 cup raisins
1 cup mini pretzels
1 cup cocktail peanuts
1 cup candy-covered chocolate pieces

Mix together; place in bowl and serve.
Also great to give in jars as gifts.

Day 330

Dark Chocolate Peppermint Bark
. . . .

1 (16 ounce) package dark chocolate candy melts
½ teaspoon peppermint extract
6 candy canes, crushed

*Melt chocolate according to package instructions.
Add extract and stir. Pour melted chocolate onto
cookie sheet lined with waxed paper and spread
evenly. Sprinkle candy cane pieces onto chocolate
and gently press down. Refrigerate until set.
Break into pieces. Store in airtight
container in refrigerator.*

Day 331

Chocolate Crescent Bars
. . . .

1 (8 ounce) tube crescent rolls
⅔ cup butter
⅓ cup light brown sugar
1 cup chopped pecans
1 (12 ounce) package milk chocolate chips

Press crescent rolls onto ungreased jelly-roll pan pinching together to seal. In a saucepan, melt butter and sugar. Pour over crust and sprinkle with pecans. Bake at 375 degrees for 13 to 15 minutes or until golden brown. Remove from oven and sprinkle with chocolate chips. Use knife to swirl the chocolate chips as they melt.

Day 332

Chocolate–Covered Peanuts
. . . .

2 cups milk chocolate chips
1 cup semisweet chocolate chips
1 to 2 cups cocktail peanuts

Melt chocolate and stir in nuts.
Drop by spoonful onto waxed paper
and allow to cool.

Day 333

Tasty Cinnamon Sticks

. . . .

For a wonderful addition to a hot chocolate
drink, try cinnamon sticks. Even better, dip your
cinnamon sticks in melted chocolate and let them
dry before using them to stir your drink.

**FROM *IN THE KITCHEN WITH
MARY & MARTHA: COOKIN' UP CHRISTMAS***

Day 334

Chocolate Snowballs
. . . .

1¼ cups butter
⅔ cup sugar
1 teaspoon vanilla extract
2 cups flour
⅛ teaspoon salt
½ cup cocoa powder, unsweetened
2 cups pecans, chopped
½ cup powdered sugar

*In a medium bowl, cream butter and sugar
until light and fluffy. Stir in vanilla. Sift together
flour, salt, and cocoa; stir into creamed mixture.
Mix in pecans until well blended. Cover,
and chill for at least 2 hours. Roll chilled dough
into 1-inch balls. Place on ungreased cookie sheets
about 2 inches apart. Bake at 350 degrees
for 20 minutes in preheated oven.
Roll in powdered sugar when cooled.*

Day 335

Candy Bar Crescents
· · · · · · · · · · · · · · · ·

8 regular-sized chocolate
caramel nugget candy bars
1 (8 ounce) tube refrigerated crescent rolls
½ cup melted butter

*Divide bars into eight pieces. Unroll crescent
dough and place candy bar pieces inside. Roll up
the crescents and pinch to seal. Place on a lightly
greased baking pan and brush lightly with melted
butter. Bake at 375 degrees for 8 to 10 minutes
until golden brown. Do not overbake.*

Day 336

Candy Cane Cocoa
. . . .

4 cups milk
3 (1 ounce) squares semisweet chocolate, chopped
3 peppermint candy canes, crushed
1 cup whipped topping
4 small peppermint candy canes

In a saucepan, heat milk until hot. Do not boil.
Whisk in chocolate and crushed peppermint
candies until melted and smooth. Pour hot cocoa
into mugs and top with whipped topping.
Serve with a candy cane for stirring.

Day 337

Christmas Mix
· · · · · · · · · · · · ·

2 cups peanuts, roasted and salted
1 cup red and green
candy-covered chocolate pieces
1 cup white chocolate or yogurt-covered raisins

Mix together; place in bowl and serve.

Day 338

Quality Time
. . . .

Spend some quality time with
your family this Christmas season. Cook up
a special dinner of family favorites and enjoy
a delicious chocolate dessert while watching
a great Christmas classic on TV.

**FROM *IN THE KITCHEN WITH
MARY & MARTHA: COOKIN' UP CHRISTMAS***

Day 339

White Chocolate
Caramel Pecan Bites
. . . .

3 cups white chocolate chips
1 cup pecans
1 cup caramel baking balls

Melt chocolate and stir in other ingredients.
Drop by spoonful onto waxed paper,
and let set up in refrigerator.

Day 340

Chocolate Peanut Clusters
· ·

2 tablespoons creamy peanut butter
1 cup semisweet chocolate chips
1 cup butterscotch chips
2 cups salted peanuts

*In medium saucepan, combine peanut
butter and chocolate and butterscotch chips.
Cook over medium heat until chips are
melted and smooth. Remove from heat
and add peanuts. Drop by rounded
spoonfuls onto waxed paper.*

Day 341

Chocolate Spice Cookies
. . . .

1 box spice cake mix
2 eggs
½ cup vegetable oil
1 cup milk chocolate chips

*Preheat oven to 350 degrees.
Combine all ingredients in bowl and
mix well with spoon. Drop by heaping
tablespoons onto ungreased cookie sheet.
Bake for 8 to 10 minutes. Do not overbake.
Remove to wire rack to cool.*

Day 342

White Chocolate Lemon Cake
. . . .
1 box yellow cake mix, prepared
1 (4 ounce) box white chocolate
instant pudding, prepared
1 (4 ounce) box lemon instant pudding, prepared
1 (8 ounce) container frozen
whipped topping, thawed

*Cut cake into serving sizes and place into serving
bowls. Layer with white chocolate pudding,
then lemon pudding, and then whipped topping.*

Day 343

Festive Rocky Road Bites
. . . .

½ cup heavy whipping cream
1 (12 ounce) package milk chocolate chips
3 cups colored mini marshmallows
2 cups peanuts

Heat whipping cream in a saucepan over medium-high heat for 2 minutes until bubbles appear. Remove from heat. Add chocolate chips and stir until smooth. Allow to cool for 8 to 10 minutes, stirring occasionally. Add marshmallows and stir to coat. Stir in peanuts until covered. Drop by tablespoonfuls onto waxed paper and cool.

Day 344

Peppermint Twist
White Hot Chocolate
· · · · · · · · · · · · · · · · ·

4 cups milk
3 ounces white chocolate, chopped
⅓ cup red-and-white-striped candy canes
or hard peppermint candies, crushed
⅛ teaspoon salt
Whipped topping
Additional red-and-white-striped
candy canes, crushed

Bring milk to a simmer in saucepan.
Reduce heat to medium-low. Add white chocolate,
crushed candy, and salt; whisk until smooth.
Ladle into mugs, dividing equally. Serve with
whipped topping and additional crushed candy.

Day 345

Light Chocolate Icing

1 (3 ounce) box instant chocolate pudding
1 cup cold milk
½ teaspoon vanilla
½ cup shortening
½ cup butter
¾ cup sugar

*Mix pudding, milk, and vanilla for 2 minutes
with a wire whisk. In a separate bowl,
combine remaining ingredients. Fold into
pudding mix and blend well.*

Day 346

Peanut Butter Hot Chocolate
· ·

1 envelope instant hot chocolate mix
2 tablespoons creamy peanut butter

*Prepare hot chocolate according to
directions on packet. Stir in peanut butter.*

Day 347

Mom's Christmas Shortbread
· ·
(FROM THE KITCHEN OF SARAH REID)

1 cup unsalted butter,
  softened
1 egg yolk
1 teaspoon vanilla
½ cup powdered sugar

2 cups flour
Christmas sprinkles
Colored sugar
Chocolate chips

Preheat oven to 325 degrees. In bowl, cream butter, egg yolk, and vanilla. Sift powdered sugar and flour into creamed mixture. Mix to form workable dough. Roll out and cut into shapes with cookie cutters. Place cookies on ungreased cookie sheets. Decorate with sprinkles, colored sugar, or chocolate chips, or leave plain. Bake for 20 minutes. Cookies should not brown. Let cool completely on sheets.

Day 348

Spicy Hot Cocoa

. . . .

2 cups milk
½ teaspoon allspice
4 to 5 tablespoons chocolate syrup
Whipped topping

*Warm milk in small saucepan. Add allspice
and chocolate syrup until heated through.
Serve in a mug and top with whipped topping.*

Day 349

Peanut Butter Chocolate Kisses
· · · · · · · · · · · · · · · · · · · ·

1 cup butter, softened
1 cup peanut butter
1 cup sugar
1 cup brown sugar
2 eggs
2 teaspoons vanilla

3½ cups flour
2 teaspoons baking soda
1 teaspoon salt
Additional sugar
1 (16 ounce) package
   chocolate candy Kisses

*Combine butter, peanut butter, and sugars;
blend until creamy. Add eggs and vanilla; blend.
Mix flour, baking soda, and salt. Add to creamed
mixture; mix well. Shape dough into balls and roll
in sugar. Bake at 350 degrees for 7 minutes.
Place Kiss in center of each cookie 2 to 3 minutes
after removing from oven*

Chocolate Christmas Truffles
. . . .

⅔ cup heavy whipping cream
2 cups semisweet or milk chocolate chips
2 teaspoons vanilla

COATING:

Cocoa
Flaked coconut
Toffee bits

Chopped nuts
Christmas sprinkles

*In saucepan, heat cream almost to a boil.
Remove from heat and add chocolate chips.
Whisk gently until chocolate is melted and
mixture is smooth. Stir in vanilla and pour into
bowl. Cover and refrigerate for 3 hours or until
firm. Coating: When chocolate mixture is firm,
scoop into 1-inch balls and roll in coatings.
Cover and refrigerate for 2 hours. Serve cold.
Keep refrigerated in airtight container.
Makes approximately 30 truffles.*

Day 351

Chocolate-Dipped Candy Canes

Spruce up some candy canes for the chocolate
lover in your life. Melt ½ cup of semisweet
chocolate chips and 2 tablespoons of shortening
in a saucepan over low heat until smooth.
Dip 16 candy canes in the chocolate (leaving out
the bottom quarter of the stick for handling).
Lay on waxed paper to cool for approximately
2 minutes, then roll chocolate-covered ends in
festive-colored sprinkles or mini chocolate chips.
Store loosely covered for up to two weeks.

Day 352

Pretzel Wreaths
· · · · · · · · · · · · · ·

1 (16 ounce) package white or
milk chocolate candy melts
Almond or peppermint extract (optional)
1 bag small pretzel twists
Christmas sprinkles

*Melt chocolate, adding a few drops almond or
peppermint extract if desired. Dip rounded
bottoms of five pretzels into chocolate. Lay pretzels
on waxed paper in a circle with sides touching and
chocolate edges toward center. Repeat and place
second circle on top of first, slightly staggered.
Decorate wreath with sprinkles.
Allow to cool completely before packaging.*

Day 353

Festive Holiday Bark
. . . .

16 ounces vanilla-flavored candy coating
2 cups small pretzel twists
½ cup red and green candy-coated chocolate

*Line a cookie sheet with waxed paper
or parchment paper. Place candy coating
in a microwave-safe bowl. Microwave for 2½
minutes. Stir; microwave at 30-second intervals
until completely melted and smooth. Place pretzels
and candy-coated chocolate pieces in a large bowl.
Pour melted coating over and stir until well
coated. Spread onto waxed paper-lined baking
sheet. Let stand until firm or place in
refrigerator to set up faster. Store in
a container at room temperature.*

Day 354

Sandy's Christmas Truffles
(FROM THE KITCHEN OF SANDRA SWEENY SILVER)

3 cups semisweet chocolate chips
1 (14 ounce) can sweetened condensed milk
2 tablespoons butter, softened
Cocoa
Crushed nuts
Powdered sugar
Christmas sprinkles

Melt chocolate chips in double boiler. Stir in condensed milk and butter. Cook until mixture thickens. Cool until firm. Use melon-baller or teaspoon to scoop small amount of truffle mixture. Roll into ball. Dip truffles in cocoa, crushed nuts, powdered sugar, or sprinkles. Allow to set before sharing.

Day 355

Chocolate Crème Soda
. . . .
4 tablespoons chocolate syrup
1 to 2 cups club soda
2 scoops chocolate ice cream
Whipped topping

*Mix chocolate syrup with ½ cup club soda.
Add ice cream and stir. Add more club soda
to taste and top with whipped topping.*

Day 356

No-Bake Christmas Graham Fudge

2 cups semisweet chocolate chips
¼ cup butter or margarine
2½ cups graham cracker crumbs
1½ cups almonds or pecans, chopped
1 (14 ounce) can sweetened condensed milk
1 teaspoon vanilla

Melt chocolate chips and butter together until smooth. In large bowl, combine graham cracker crumbs and nuts. Stir in sweetened condensed milk and vanilla until crumbs are moistened, then stir in chocolate mixture until mixed. Pat evenly into greased 9x13-inch baking pan. Let stand at room temperature for 2 hours before cutting into squares.

Day 357

Snowy Cinnamon Cocoa
. . . .

4 cups milk
1 cup chocolate syrup
1 teaspoon cinnamon
Whipped topping
¼ cup semisweet chocolate chips

Place milk and chocolate syrup in microwavable
bowl and stir. Cook on high for 3 to 4 minutes
or until hot. Stir in cinnamon. Pour into
four large mugs and garnish with
whipped topping and chocolate chips.

Day 358

Ohio Buckeyes
· · · · · · · · · · · ·

1 cup margarine, melted
2 cups peanut butter
4 cups powdered sugar
1 teaspoon vanilla
1 (2x2 inch) piece of paraffin
3 cups semisweet chocolate chips

*Cream together maragarine, peanut butter,
powdered sugar, and vanilla. Chill in refrigerator
for a few hours, then roll into balls approximately
¼ inch in diameter. Chill balls in refrigerator for
at least 8 hours. Melt paraffin and chocolate in
double boiler. Using toothpick, dip each ball into
chocolate mixture, twirling off excess chocolate.
Place on waxed paper to set up.*

Day 359

Reindeer Food
. . . .

10 cups crispy cereal squares
1¼ cups white chocolate chips
½ cup peanut butter
¼ cup butter
½ teaspoon vanilla
1½ cups powdered sugar

*Put cereal in large bowl. In saucepan,
melt chocolate chips, peanut butter, and butter.
Remove from heat and add vanilla. Pour mixture
over cereal and toss. Add powdered sugar to bowl
and toss until cereal is well coated. Turn out on
cookie sheets lined with waxed paper to cool.*

Day 360

Chocolate Pound Cake
. . . .

1 box chocolate cake mix
1 small box instant chocolate pudding mix
1¾ cups milk
2 eggs
1 bag mini chocolate chips
Powdered sugar

Preheat oven to 350 degrees. In large bowl,
combine all ingredients except powdered sugar
and beat by hand. Bake for 1 hour.
Dust with powdered sugar.

Day 361

Peppermint Pieces
. . . .

16 ounces white chocolate chips
4 ounces peppermint candy canes, crushed

*In small saucepan over low heat, melt white
chocolate chips, stirring until smooth.
Add crushed peppermint. Pour mixture
onto waxed paper–lined baking sheet.
Freeze until set. Break into pieces.*

Day 362

Chocolate Cheese Ball
· · · · · · · · · · · · · · · · · · · ·

1 (8 ounce) package cream cheese, softened
¼ cup unsalted butter, softened
¼ cup peanut butter
¾ cup powdered sugar
2 tablespoons light brown sugar
3 tablespoons cocoa
½ cup mini chocolate chips
⅔ cup finely chopped pecans, toasted

*In medium bowl, beat cream cheese, butter,
and peanut butter until creamy. Stir in powdered
sugar, brown sugar, cocoa, and chocolate chips.
Cover and chill for at least 2 hours or until firm.
Shape mixture into ball and roll in chopped
pecans. Cover and chill until ready
to serve. Serve with graham crackers.*

Day 363

Chocolate Eggnog
. . . .

8 egg yolks
1 cup sugar
4 cups whole milk
½ cup semisweet chocolate chips
2 teaspoons vanilla extract

Beat egg yolks and sugar until thick.
In a large saucepan, add milk and chocolate chips.
Bring to a boil. Remove from heat and beat in
egg yolk mix. Stir in the vanilla and serve.

Day 364

Snowmen Cookies
. . . .

White chocolate almond bark
Nutter Butter sandwich cookies
Mini semisweet chocolate chips

Melt almond bark and spread on cookies.
Place two mini chocolate chips
side by side to make eyes.

Day 365

Every Good Gift

. . . .

Every good and perfect gift is
from above, coming down from the
Father of the heavenly lights.

JAMES 1:17

Notes........Favourites...................................

Chocolate Pecan Tassies 239

....

....

....

....

....

....

....

....

....

....

....

....

....

....

....

....

....

....

....

....

....

....

Notes   To try

Earthquake cake 303
Chocolate Chai 82
Snickerdoodle cake 61

Notes..
....
....
....
....
....
....
....
....
....
....
....

Notes..
....
....
....
....
....
....
....
....
....
....
....
....

....
....
....
....
....
....
....
....
....
....
....
....

Notes...
....
....
....
....
....
....
....
....
....
....
....

Notes..
....
....
....
....
....
....
....
....
....
....
....

Notes..
....
....
....
....
....
....
....
....
....
....
....
....